THE DIGITAL REAL ESTATE MARKETING PLAYBOOK

How to generate more leads, close more sales, and even become a millionaire realtor with the power of internet marketing

Nick Tsai

SPECIAL BONUSES FOR YOU

Thanks for getting this book. Please check the following resources to take your real estate marketing to the next level.

1. Download Your Free Real Estate Marketing Checklist

This checklist features 86 marketing tips to generate more leads online & offline.

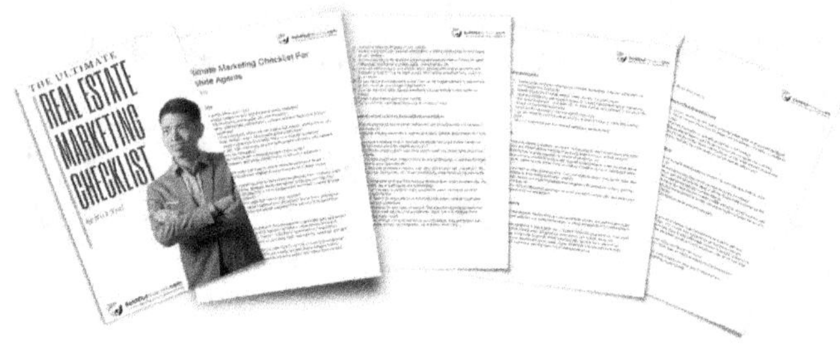

Download your free checklist at
https://soldouthouses.com/checklist .

2. Join our "Sold Out Houses Pro" membership and get access to our library of real estate marketing tools, templates, and swipe files.

Try it for free at https://soldouthouses.com/vip/

TESTIMONIALS FROM MY CLIENTS

"I'm so impressed with the quality of the work! Nick is consistently in overdrive, and that's something you don't find in everybody; I highly recommend you reach out to Nick for help."

~ Kendell Linden

"Nick Tsai is fantastic...he happily answers all my questions and gets my website optimized. It's an awesome service, and I highly recommend it!"

~ Tony Lander

"Nick gave me lots of valuable resources and advice to help me out. He also shared many marketing tips that gave me so much clarity about what to do to grow my business."

~ Anne Tsai

"Nick was very helpful and gave me lots of clarity on my keyword strategy ... he was very responsive to my questions and the turnaround was really fast!"

~ Gina Couper

"Nick Tsai is a nice guy and he is easy to work with. And I'm sure he has the knowledge and expertise to help you with your marketing questions."

~ Laura Whittenberger

"Nick is one of the best SEO mentors and I learned a lot about SEO from him."

~ Davida Huang

TABLE OF CONTENTS

INTRODUCTION 1

WHY MOST REAL ESTATE AGENTS STRUGGLE TO GET NEW CLIENTS 7

They Fail to Market Effectively Online 7

Other Reasons Real Estate Agents Struggle to Bring in New Clients 9

How to Attract New Clients Online 10

6 MYTHS ABOUT DIGITAL REAL ESTATE MARKETING 12

Myth #1: Digital Marketing Isn't Needed 13

Myth #2: It Costs Too Much Money 13

Myth #3: It's Too Competitive 14

Myth #4: It's Okay to Wait Until Next Year or the Year After 15

Myth #5: It Doesn't Work 15

Myth #6: Cheaper Digital Marketing Services Are Just as Good 16

Allow Us to Show You the Effectiveness of Digital Marketing 17

THE OLD WAY VS. NEW WAY OF REAL ESTATE MARKETING ... 18

Newspapers 18

Direct Mail Campaigns 19

Yellow Pages 20

Word of Mouth 21

Cold Calling 22

Flyers 23

TRADE IN OLD MARKETING FOR NEW MARKETING 25

THE SOLUTION: THE S.W.I.F.T. METHOD 26

Social Media in the S.W.I.F.T. Method 27

Website in the S.W.I.F.T. Method 28

Information in the S.W.I.F.T. Method 28

Funnel in the S.W.I.F.T. Method 29

Traffic in the S.W.I.F.T. Method 30

How We Help Realtors Bring in New Leads.. 30

SOCIAL MEDIA 31

Tips to Do Social Media Marketing: 33

Social Media Optimization... 43

How to Optimize Your Social Media Profile 44

The Importance of Optimizing Your Social Media Profile Regularly ... 46

WEBSITE 48

How to Design a Website to Generate More Leads 51

How to Optimize Your Website to Generate More Leads From Google
.... 54

What Is SEO Marketing in the Real Estate Industry?.............................. 55

Why Do You Need to Do SEO? 55

What Are the Benefits of SEO to Real Estate Agents? 56

How to Ensure the Best SEO Marketing Results 58

How Search Engines Work... 59

How Does Google Decide to Rank Content? 59

#1. The Content on Your Website Pages 60

#2. The Proper Use of Popular Keywords... 60

#3. The Length and Quality of Your Blog Content.................................. 61

#4. The Loading Times for Your Website 62

#5. A Mobile-Friendly Structure 62

#6. The Time Visitors Spend on Your Website 62

#7. The Inbound Links or Backlinks to Your Website............................. 63

The Importance of Keyword Research... 64

How to Optimize Your Site with Keyword Phrases................................. 65

Optimizing Additional Pages 66

Add Content Regularly to Increase Traffic.. 67

Get Started and Do Not Stop 67

Steps to Rank Your Website Better 68

Tips for Successful Search Engine Optimization 68

#1: Claim Your Google My Business Listing 68

#2: Optimize with Local Keywords 69

#3: Encourage Reviews 69

#4: Provide Valuable Information on Your Website 70

#5: Use Social Media 70

#6: Update Website as Needed 71

#7: Build Citations 71

#8: Building Backlinks 72

SEO Marketing Takes Time, Knowledge, and Effort 72

How to Get Help with SEO 74

Contact Us for Help with Website Optimization 75

INFORMATION 76

How to Use Content to Position Yourself and Get More Clients 76

Content Is King 78

What Type of Content Can You Publish? 79

Articles 79

Images 80

Videos 82

50 Most Engaging Content Types to Publish on Social Media 83

Create Content and Promote It 103

Need Help with Content Creation? 104

FUNNEL 105

How Realtors Use Email Marketing to Generate New Clients 112

Two Journeys for Customers 114

Getting Help with Feeding Your Funnel 116

TRAFFIC 119

Paid Traffic vs. Organic Traffic 119

Take Advantage of Paid Traffic 120

Know Your Numbers 120

Use Split Testing to Optimize Your Ads 122

Turn Your Leads into Lifetime Clients 122

Which Types of Ads Can You Use? 123

#1. Search Ads: 123

Google Ads 124

How to Set Up a Search Ad 125

#2. Display Ads: 126

How to Set Up a Display Ad 127

#3. Social Ads: 128

How You Can Set Up a Social Media Ad 128

1. Facebook Ads: 129

2. Instagram Ads: 130

3. YouTube Ads: 131

4. Remarketing Ads: 131

How to Set Up a Remarketing Ad 133

5. Click-to-Call Ads: 133

6. Call-Only Ads: 134

7. Google Map Ads: 134

Other Ways to Send Traffic to Your Website 135

CONTACT US FOR HELP WITH GENERATING TRAFFIC 137

SPECIAL BONUS: WOULD YOU LIKE OUR TEAM TO DESIGN A CUSTOM MARKETING PLAN FOR YOU FREE? 138

RESOURCES 141

INTRODUCTION

This book is your road map to generate more leads, get more clients, and grow your real estate business to the next level.

If you are reading this book, chances are you are looking for new ways to grow your business.

- Maybe because you want to achieve your financial goal
- Maybe because you want more freedom for what you love
- Maybe because you want a better life for your family

And trust me, no matter what your dream is this book will change your life.

I know it sounds like a bold statement, and you may be a little skeptical.

You may have bought many marketing books and courses and feel confused and overwhelmed.

You may also have tried some of the "marketing hacks" for your business but got no results.

I understand your pain, and I have been there.

I used to spend tens of thousands of dollars on courses and seminars that sold nothing but pipe dreams.

I also hired agencies to help me with my business which burned up my marketing budget with no results.

Trust me, if you are struggling to get more leads online. It is not your fault. **There is simply too much misleading information.**

Some false gurus try to sell high-ticket courses but never run a real business. And some unethical agencies want to sell you services they never apply to their own businesses.

These people do more harm than good to businesses and give a bad name to legitimate marketers.

This book is not one of those associated with the B.S.

What I will share with you in this book **is what works for my clients and me.**

I will show you the S.W.I.F.T. framework I am using to build, grow, and scale both me and my clients' businesses online.

And every time I start a new business, I build the same system for myself.

If you read the entire book to the end, you will have a clear blueprint about what to do next to bring your business to the next level.

But first, read this disclaimer.

This book is not another "get rich quick" scheme, and do not expect to achieve overnight success. Internet marketing is a marathon; it takes time and effort to reap the reward.

What I ask of you is to implement what you learn in your business.

But **do not take everything I say blindly**. Online marketing is ever-changing, and some tactics in this book may become outdated. And my experience and opinions are not always right for everyone as well.

Instead, use my book as a roadmap to find the right direction. But test everything, and let the market reveal what is working right now.

And if you implement the tips I'm sharing with you to your business and be persistent with it, you will see great results.

By now, you may be wondering, "Why should I listen to you?"

So let me briefly introduce myself.

My Story

My name is Nick Tsai. I became a realtor when I was 25 and started my online businesses when I was 27. I have been running online businesses for 10 years, and I help many owners grow and scale their businesses with the power of internet marketing.

I founded https://soldouthouses.com, a website that helps real estate agents get more leads and grow their businesses with the power of digital marketing.

My team and I have had great success with helping my clients with digital marketing.

But it all started quite humbly.

Ten years ago, I became a real estate agent.

As a rookie in that industry, I struggled getting clients.

I followed all the traditional advice from the industry.

Distributing flyers
Posting classified ads
Cold calling
Cold mailing

But nothing seemed to work.

I was frustrated, struggling, and hopeless.

I worked 12 hours a day, every day.

And still got no clients.

I eventually burned out and quit.

I lost my confidence and started doubting myself.

Those were the worst days of my life.

Until one day, I received a phone call that changed everything.

It was from a stranger who wanted me to help him sell his house.

I never called him, I never mailed him, and I didn't even know who he was.

But for some reason, he had found my website.

It was an ugly blog I used as a personal notebook where I wrote down everything I learned about real estate.

And for some unknown reason, it became the #1 ranking real estate blog in my local area.

In the next few months, people called, asked me questions about real estate, and even begged me to accept them as clients.

All of a sudden, I became the go-to expert in the local area.

And getting clients became effortless.

It was an aha moment for me.

I realized

"It's easier to attract clients than to chase clients."

In the past, I tried to get new clients by chasing after them...

...by cold calling, cold mailing, and sending flyers (junk mail). I became an annoying salesperson.

But with the power of the internet, I could easily reach people who were ready to buy and position myself as an expert!

So, I decided to dive into internet marketing to discover how I could attract more clients online.

I studied countless marketing books, attended marketing seminars, and learned from the best marketing experts in the world.

I discovered a very powerful framework called S.W.I.F.T., to grow my business and get great results for my clients.

And in this book, I'm going to give you the blueprint to implement this framework.

Thank you for taking time to read my story!

If you follow the secrets I will be sharing with you, you *too* can build a successful business, no matter your starting point or the industry you are in.

If you want to learn more about how to bring your real estate business to the next level, go to https://soldouthouses.com

WHY MOST REAL ESTATE AGENTS STRUGGLE TO GET NEW CLIENTS

Most real estate agents struggle to get new clients. Understanding why can help agents switch gears so they bring in more leads than they can handle.

They Fail to Market Effectively Online

Approximately 76.2 percent or 290 million Americans accessed the internet in 2016. Out of these people, there were about 1.17 billion searches on Google for information. What are they searching for? Just about anything they want to know, including where to find a good realtor.

Most people who need a real estate agent will ask family or friends. If their friends speak highly of a realtor, they will likely research the agent online.

This method of bringing in new clients has a lot to do with the positive experience you provide your clients. Word of mouth is still one of the best ways to grow a business.

But what happens when a prospect has friends who are not exactly happy with their agent or don't want to ask their friends? That's when people turn to Google to find one.

People will search for one of these phrases on Google:

- Realtor near me
- Real estate agent in <city>
- realtor in <city>
- realty companies in <city>
- realty companies near me
- best real estate broker

If you do not show up in search results, you're going to have a difficult time bringing in new leads.

Now, if you come up on the first page of Google's search results, and you still don't bring in new clients, there's something else going on.

You are not active online. It's important to be active online because people want to know you care about your clients inside AND outside the office. This means you should have active social media accounts and a regularly updated website blog. The more people see you online, the more likely they will make an appointment with you.

You fail to funnel them correctly. Funneling is a marketing term that means advertising to a large group of people and then bringing them through promotions that will leave you with just the people who will convert into new leads.

Other Reasons Real Estate Agents Struggle to Bring in New Clients

Besides not marketing effectively online, realtors also struggle to bring in new clients because they miss opportunities to do so. Often, it is missing new clients' phone calls.

When a potential client calls to make an appointment, that person wants to do it at that time. If no one answers, that person will likely just call the next agent instead of leaving a message. All missed calls are missed opportunities for new clients, so it's important to employ a system to keep missed calls at a minimum.

Inexperienced staff or poor customer service are two other reasons many potential clients go with a different realtor.

When a potential client calls for an appointment or for information, the agent who answers gives off the first impression.

If that first impression is not a good one, the person will simply call the next agent. Therefore, it's highly important the agent answers the phone in a friendly, personable manner and has the information the client requests.

Even if the agent doesn't have all the answers, that person should seek an answer and assure the caller the information is forthcoming. If the agent must call the potential client back, it must be done in as little time as possible. Potential clients want a realtor who is responsive to their needs and calling in with a question is a good test.

Missed calls and customer service problems are two issues that can decrease the number of new clients you receive in a year, but they are not the problems that cause you the most struggle in your business.

Increasing the effectiveness of online marketing can boost your new client numbers month after month and year after year.

How to Attract New Clients Online

Failing with online marketing is the reason most real estate agents struggle to bring in new clients. These agents either don't have good visibility, have a bad reputation, or are inactive online.

The good news is these three problems are easily fixed. Realtors have only to employ a process called S.W.I.F.T.

This process helps realtors bring in new clients by increasing social media visibility, creating a website that attracts potential clients, providing valuable information, funneling people through the marketing pipeline, and boosting traffic.

S.W.I.F.T. stands for

- **S**ocial media
- **W**ebsite
- **I**nformation
- **F**unnel
- **T**raffic

Social media is where you will share information about yourself, your office, and the services you provide to local people who are using social media.

The website portion of the equation is developing your site in a way that not only attracts people but also makes them want to call you for an appointment.

The information step means providing valuable information to help people use you as their realtor.

The funnel helps bring many potential clients to you and then weeds out the ones that will not end up making an appointment.

T is for traffic, and the more traffic you bring in, the more success you will have bringing in new clients.

S.W.I.F.T. is a proven method of bringing in new real estate clients. It has been tested on many real estate agents, and they have all reported dramatic increases in new lead numbers.

It takes some time to learn this method. The following information will help you understand each part of the process.

Once you succeed with one part, it will make the next one much easier. Jumping around isn't the best way to use this method of online marketing. But eventually it all works together to bring in new traffic continuously so you can grow your business for many years.

6 MYTHS ABOUT DIGITAL REAL ESTATE MARKETING

As a digital marketing agency, we have heard many myths about online marketing to bring new clients to businesses.

It's unfortunate many realtors believe these objections because they are missing out on effective and lucrative sources for new leads.

Knowing the myths and why they are untrue can help realtors get past them and take advantage of the best way to market their businesses.

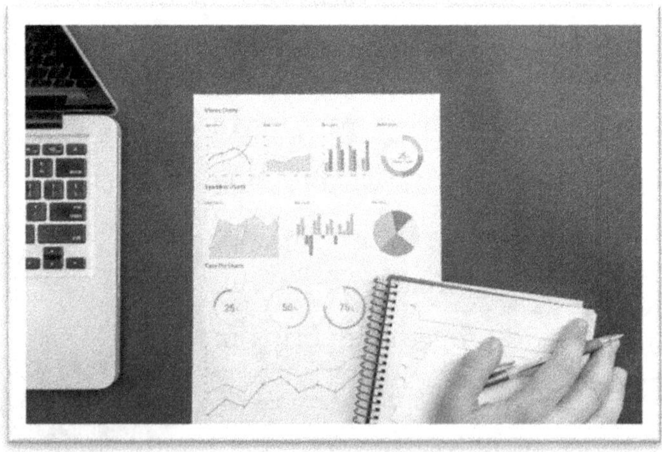

Myth #1: Digital Marketing Isn't Needed

Digital marketing is needed more than ever. Fifty-one percent of consumers search for realtors on search engines. So if you think about it, just over half of all people who need a real estate agent look online first to find one.

Digital marketing makes it possible for you to appear to those people searching for real estate agents. When you have a website and are active on social media, people will see you and be more likely to call for an appointment.

Myth #2: It Costs Too Much Money

How much is a client worth to you? Think about it for a minute.

If a digital marketing agency could bring you just one new client in a month, would that income pay for the services? What about if the agency brought you two new clients or more?

With any type of marketing, you must think about the Return on Investment (ROI). This is what makes it worth it.

An effective digital marketing strategy, like the one we use called S.W.I.F.T., can bring in new clients who would end up paying for our services plus make you the money you otherwise wouldn't make because you didn't market online.

So, does it really matter if it "costs too much" when it brings in more money than you are spending?

Myth #3: It's Too Competitive

Competition is always present in a business. It's not about your competitors, though. It's about what you do to get to clients before they do. What you're doing now may not be working, so you must try something else.

One thing is for sure, you will not beat out your competition by doing nothing. Also, the longer you wait, the harder it will be to come out on top.

With digital marketing, you have two parts at work: organic and paid.

Organic digital marketing is free and grows slowly. It involves adding quality content to your site, being active on social media, and utilizing other ways to improve your business's visibility online.

Paid digital marketing involves paying for ads on Google, Facebook, and other websites. This form of marketing is more expensive but provides fast results. Organic is free and will bring results over time.

Implementing both and adjusting how much you spend on ads as your organic leads increase can bring you new clients for the lowest cost per lead.

Myth #4: It's Okay to Wait Until Next Year or the Year After

You could wait until next year or the year after, but by that time your competitors will be quite happy with the hundreds of new clients they brought into their businesses because you delayed digital marketing.

They will also be way ahead, which means it could take you months to see results or a lot of money to see leads come in with paid ads. Just because digital marketing will still be around next year and the year after, doesn't mean you should wait that long. Do you really want to give up the opportunity to bring in new clients now? That's what you'll be doing if you wait.

Myth #5: It Doesn't Work

It doesn't work if you don't work it correctly.

Many real estate agents try to do digital marketing themselves, and when they don't see results, they give up. Most of the time, it's because those realtors do not know how to do digital marketing correctly.

Like most types of marketing, it takes knowledge, skill, and experience to do it the right way.

It can take months or even years to know how to run ad campaigns effectively. There are details you may be missing that could hurt your results a great deal.

The same goes for website development, content creation, and search engine marketing. It's a lot to handle on your own while you run your business.

Keeping up with the latest changes in internet marketing also takes a great deal of effort. This is why digital marketers have a job.

Yes, digital marketing may not work, but that's only because it's not done the right way. When you have a professional running your digital marketing campaign, you will see how well it works

Myth #6: Cheaper Digital Marketing Services Are Just as Good

You get what you pay for when it comes to digital marketing.

When you go with a digital marketing agency that charges little for its services, you end up with people without the knowledge, experience, and skills needed to perform online marketing effectively. This wastes money because you will pay them for not bringing in leads.

It is better to pay a bit more money for good digital marketing services and make money off new clients. Investing in good digital marketing pays for itself.

Allow Us to Show You the Effectiveness of Digital Marketing

Our digital marketing strategy consists of something we call S.W.I.F.T. This stands for social media, website, information, funnel, and traffic.

We start with setting up social network accounts for our clients and then managing them to bring leads to their website. Their website is also managed by us. We make sure it's not only functional but attractive.

To help with search engine rankings, we add quality content consistently. This information is what funnels people interested in your services to the site. Once on the site, we convert them with effective calls to action.

Contact us at https://soldouthouses.com today for more information about our online marketing packages. We would love to show you how effective our proven digital marketing strategy is for real estate agents.

You can also sign up for our Sold Out Houses Pro membership which gives you all the marketing tools and templates you need to succeed with real estate marketing. You can go to https://soldouthouses.com/vip to sign up for your 14-days free trial.

THE OLD WAY VS. NEW WAY OF REAL ESTATE MARKETING

Real estate marketing has changed over the years. Understanding how it has changed and keeping up with those changes is what we help you do to continue running a successful business.

The following are some of the many ways real estate marketing has changed over the years.

Newspapers

Realtors can still put an ad in the local paper for their services, but it's unlikely they will receive the same results they once did.

People simply don't turn to local papers for news anymore. Instead, they tap a couple of times on their smartphones to read the latest news for the local area and beyond.

This is why realty companies have abandoned newspaper ads and put their money into ones online.

Online ads are much more successful now because there are approximately 312 million Americans using the internet. A wider audience means more exposure, which is exactly what you want when you market your business.

It's true that your target audience is a fraction of the total population online since your realty office only interests people in your local area.

However, with so many people online across the nation, it's fair to say that people in your local area are using the internet more than a newspaper.

Direct Mail Campaigns

Sending postcards to people in your local area worked well in the past. Now, it's not as effective.

One in five people throws away direct mail unopened. As disheartening as this sounds, if you've invested money recently in direct mail, it's something you must know so you can use your money effectively.

Direct mail campaigns have been replaced with email, text messages, blogs, and social media.

When you have a message to send to a large volume of people, use one of those options. Past clients should receive an email or text message. Prospects should receive messages via your blog or social media.

People are using mobile devices more than ever, so opening an email, text message, or seeing a social media post on their feed works well for them.

Those who are interested in hiring a real estate agent will check their blogs for specials and information. This is the new way to market your service.

Yellow Pages

Buying space in the Yellow Pages used to be an effective and expensive way to market your business.

It was the best way to put your services in front of the eyes of people specifically looking for a real estate agent.

But the Yellow Pages book is not delivered to most people anymore. People stopped using them because of the internet.

Yes, the internet replaced the Yellow Pages in many ways. Now, all the directories people need for local services are on a search engine or an online directory.

In marketing, you must follow where people go, and they are online. This means you now must buy ad space on search engines, websites, and social networks. It also means adding your business information (name, address, and phone number) to online directories, such as www.yellowpages.com.

Word of Mouth

Word of mouth used to be one of the best ways to market your business, and guess what? It still is! It is just different now.

You can still gain referrals from people when they boast about how satisfied they are with your services, but often, it is done online with reviews.

Besides people telling each other face-to-face, they leave reviews on Google, Facebook, and other review sites. They want to let other people know about their experiences, good or bad.

By adding in online reviews, word-of-mouth marketing can reach many more people. Encouraging your clients to leave an online review for you is a great way to increase your credibility.

Cold Calling

You may not have done this, but many agents did something to bring back inactive leads or solicit brand new ones.

Unfortunately, with all the junk calls people receive now, getting a call from a realtor is not something they appreciate.

Cold calling has been replaced with social media in many ways. Social media ads make it possible for realtors to invite users to visit their website to learn more about their services and make an appointment.

These ads are put right in front of social media users who have already either visited the agent's website or have performed a search related to buying or selling houses.

This is called target advertising because you can select who sees the ads just like you could select who you called from a leads list.

Flyers

Flyers have fallen to the wayside as well for real estate marketing. They are often tossed into a nearby trash can or folded up and stuffed into a purse or pocket, never to be seen again.

Landing pages are today's flyers. They are web pages with one mission: to convince people they need the advertised service and to call the real estate agent to make an appointment.

See how similar landing pages are to flyers now?

A landing page is just one page, and most web designers can make one easily. The copy must be engaging and powerful. It should state the problem the person has, the solutions to the problem, and then a way to contact the real estate agent.

TRADE IN OLD MARKETING FOR NEW MARKETING

If you're still investing in old marketing tactics, you're wasting money.

It's time to invest in a new, more effective type of advertising – digital marketing. With digital marketing services, you can take advantage of all the ways to grow your brand awareness online. This includes a website that contains information about you, your staff, and the services you provide; a blog to relay messages to current and prospective clients; social media to stay in touch with people in your local community; and paid online ads to get in front of those specifically searching for your services.

Our real estate marketing team has a proven yet effective digital marketing strategy called S.W.I.F.T. (social media, website, information, funnel, and traffic) to improve online visibility and leads for realtors and realty offices. We would love to help you harness the power of the internet to bring new clients to your business. visit our site at https://soldouthouses.com for learn more about our products and services.

THE SOLUTION: THE S.W.I.F.T. METHOD

As we've said, our proven method of digital marketing has helped many realtors gain leads. We knew that realtors were having a hard time and not getting the help they needed, so we moved forward with a better solution.

In our last article, we discussed some reasons real estate agents struggle to get new clients. To recap, it's hard to get new clients because:

- Online visibility is low.
- Reviews are not online, or they are not good.
- They are inactive online.
- They are not funneling their traffic correctly.

Three out of four reasons are due to not being effective with online marketing. This is why it's imperative agents become more active in their digital marketing efforts.

The best way to do this is with the S.W.I.F.T. method.

Again, that stands for:

- Social Media

- Website
- Information
- Funnel
- Traffic

We will go more in-depth with each of these but felt it was important to provide a short overview to start.

Social Media in the S.W.I.F.T. Method

Social media is accessed by millions of people every day. This includes people in your local area. Some are looking for real estate agents, while others are looking for a new house.

People on social media often ask their followers who they recommend for a realtor, while others will just pay attention to what people say about their realtor. When you have an active Facebook and Instagram account, you will appear as in touch with people on social media.

Clients want this from their agent. They want to know that their agent is available not only when they go to the office for an appointment but also online.

It can seem like you are going above and beyond for your clients, but this is what you must do to keep a constant flow of new leads coming into your business.

Website in the S.W.I.F.T. Method

Developing a functional yet attractive website is the next step with the S.W.I.F.T. method. The website must have an aesthetically pleasing homepage that informs visitors. When people land on the page, they should be able to find what they need quickly and easily.

Most people want to find information on particular services or contact information. By displaying links to those services and your contact information on the page, you will make your visitors happy, which helps you rank on Google's search engine.

Be sure your top navigation is organized and makes it easy for people to use your site. While your page may have information on it, people are used to going up to the top right of the page to find a glossary of the site's pages.

Information in the S.W.I.F.T. Method

Providing valuable, detailed information is important in increasing trust with people. The more you teach people, the more they will want you to be their agent.

You should have content on your site in pages and posts. When you do this, you will show you are a professional in your field.

Information can also be shared on social media. When you publish posts on specific topics, you will be telling people how you performed your services and showing them a little about your personality. If they connect with the information, they will be more likely to call you for an appointment.

There's more to know about information in S.W.I.F.T., but for now just know it's an important part of being effective, relevant, and successful.

Funnel in the S.W.I.F.T. Method

The funnel is a marketing term that attracts people who are possible clients. When you attract these people, you take them through promotions to filter the ones who will make an appointment.

Funneling can be done on social media and websites. Actually, these are the channels you will use to usher people to you. When you place them in a systemic funnel, you will see more people making appointments as long as you fill the funnel with the right people.

When you use a funnel to market your business, you can expect to have new clients for not just a month or months but for years. It's a constant flow of people coming in and what comes out are new clients.

Traffic in the S.W.I.F.T. Method

Traffic is an important part of the entire S.W.I.F.T. process. It's what fills your funnel. This traffic results from what you do on social media and the website. What comes out of it are the people you want – clients.

Traffic is what you will be examining after completing the processes before it. You will find this can be the gratifying part because it shows that the efforts put into the S.W.I.F.T. method have paid off for you.

Most information on the traffic part of the S.W.I.F.T. method will be provided. Just know this is what you are working towards when you start using our digital marketing method.

How We Help Realtors Bring in New Leads

We help realtors bring in new leads by using our highly effective S.W.I.F.T. method. This marketing strategy has been used many times with success, and we are excited to bring it to so many real estate agents in the United States. If you're looking at your current marketing strategy and you're not happy with the results, try our S.W.I.F.T. method.

In the following articles, you will learn much more about our method and how to do it yourself.

We must warn you this process is difficult, and it takes a lot of time. Many real estate agents who learn how to do it our way come back to ask if we can help them with it, which we are happy to do.

SOCIAL MEDIA

As you now know, social media is the first part of the S.W.I.F.T. framework, which means promoting your personal brand and business on your fan pages, Instagram profile, Twitter profiles, and other platforms.

Social media is powerful. People use it almost daily on their cell phones and laptops. With social media, you can easily connect with anyone around your local area cheaply and affordably.

The keys to successful social media marketing are creating engaging content, connecting with your audience, and, most importantly, sharing **your personal story and life.**

For many years, I made one big mistake. I only used social media to run ads and promote my business. I never mentioned my life and personal story.

Having been timid and introverted since I was young, I wasn't comfortable with social media. If you'd seen my profile, you would notice I rarely updated it. I was always that way. When I was 10, my teacher asked me to share a story for 10 minutes; I was scared to death. I eventually stood in front of the class not saying a word the entire time. It was so embarrassing!

Even though I overcame much of my shyness as I grew up, social media was still something I didn't feel comfortable using, and, in fact, did not use.

A few years ago, I started my digital marketing agency. I struggled to get a client. Even though it was easy for me to sell a $97 product online, I couldn't sell my service.

I was frustrated, but I was not ready to quit. I decided to study those who crushed it online. I became a student of a few 8-figure entrepreneurs and reverse engineered their marketing methods.

I noticed they have one thing in common; they all have a solid personal brand, and they all share about themselves on social media.

I decided to model what they did and include social media marketing in my business. So I shared my story. I even bought ads to promote my posts. After a few months, I closed my first high-ticket client.

The power of social media is not only in its reach but also in its ability to connect.

For someone to buy from you, they need to know you, like you, and trust you. And social media offers an excellent place for someone to get to know you. Personally.

In this chapter, I will share some tips for growing your business using social media profiles, and in the "information" chapter, I will share more about content creation with you.

Tips to Do Social Media Marketing:

Here are some key social media marketing tips you can apply without having experience or expert knowledge. Just read the article carefully, and you too can get more clients.

1. Keep Content Responsive

A common mistake of many realtors is they think people still use laptops or PCs to do their important work or perform searches.

They should know times have changed, and the majority of people have switched to mobile phones for most endeavors.

Especially Google searches. Mobile phones are portable and stay in everyone's pockets.

Why wait to get to a specific spot to access the internet on a laptop?

And there's the freedom to use mobiles anywhere and anytime. So given their ease, it's what most everyone is using.

Google will show your name if you use marketing tools in the right way and have a registered brand on Google maps.

But if the site architecture is not compatible with mobile, then the prospects can not navigate to the proper information and will likely move to other agents who can accommodate them..

So make a website according to mobile architecture too. You can link your website to different social media platforms and easily view the content with a responsive architecture.

2. Consider Social Media Messaging

It is important to communicate with prospects to know their needs and what they expect from you. Many real estate agents just use social media to upload posts.

They do not check the messages and read the comments, which is not a good thing. Many social media apps allow you to have effective communication with potential clients.

The major apps for just communication purposes are WhatsApp, Telegram, Messenger, and Viber.

If you do not want to use different platforms for posting content and communication, stick to the ones you currently use.

You can chat with your clients through Instagram and Facebook as well. Without making any assumptions, try to listen to what clients say and resolve their problems.

3. Make Videos

Some real estate agents feel too shy to communicate with their prospects on social media platforms. This can become a barrier to turning their audience into clients.

But do not worry. Social media has a solution for almost all problems, even this one.

Realtors can take their time recording and editing a simple video. This allows them to connect to audiences personally and deliver the information they want to share.

In general, you can post videos on any social platform. But YouTube is probably the most popular and many people are familiar with it from watching entertainment videos. Here you can share videos related to your work and get reviews from clients.

As a bonus, you can have more organic leads by delivering a message in video form rather than text.

4. Go Live

After video, going live is the best option to promote the services. It is just like the video call but with your followers.

They have the option to write the message, and you can answer them by speaking.

Facebook and Instagram have focused on making this technology better. They allow different ads to pop up during live chat so that interested prospects can directly go to the page.

In the live video, you can show people your workplace and the equipment that you use.

Moreover, you can ask people for reviews. That way you can make changes if people have any complaints about your work and services.

5. Invest in Social Media Ads

Social media ads work just like Google ads, but the platform is different. Google ads display on the Google search results pages while social media ads display as a post.

During your regular scrolling, you can see the video that is labeled with the ad. Whether you follow the page or not, you will see the ad.

This is because of social media marketing. Invest your money in selecting social media packages that increase the reach of your posts to a high level.

6. Stay Professional

Professionalism matters a lot in every field. If you use social media, you know that every platform has a different tone. Also, they have different privacy policies.

The type of content you see on Facebook is different from Instagram. But still, there are many similarities between them.

And if you compare these to LinkedIn, you have a completely different style of professionalism.

Know the various platforms and how to interface on each one.

7. Post High Quality & Viral Content

Content marketing continues to be king in the world of digital marketing. This means you need to always post high-quality content if you want to be successful with your social media efforts.

The biggest problem marketers face when it comes to their social media engagement is they don't have time to run every aspect of their business and still develop quality content that can go viral.

Time is an essential part of any successful strategy in social media, but unfortunately, it's impossible for someone to handle everything by themselves and still get the results they expect. Successful people handle this by delegating work and hiring professionals to help them accomplish their goals.

This is also important because social media content is not just about posting the same trending news everyone is posting or creating content just to publish something every day. The only way for your posts to become relevant and viral is to make sure that everything you post is top quality.

This means coming up with fresh and useful content. For that you need to conduct market research to know what to write about. Then, you also need to ensure it's easy to understand, original, and extremely appealing in terms of textual and graphical content.

8. Have a Content Plan

When you decide to start creating content for social media, you are going to find it's extremely difficult to be consistent all year long. Even managing to generate quality content for a few weeks can prove challenging.

This is the reason you need to make a viable content plan. Of course, that's easier said than done with so many other demands when running a business.

Even so, a good content plan will be essential for you to achieve the best results, which means finding a solution that is practical and cost-effective. A content calendar is the perfect method of tracking a full year's worth of social media content suggestions.

Our team of social media marketing professionals has carefully structured this, and they ensure that each day is going to include a suggestion that is ideal based on the month and the day of the month.

9. Good Design Matters

The way your posts look is going to be just as important as the content they include. In fact, this can be more relevant in platforms like Instagram that rely on canvas-styled messages for audience engagement.

This process can also be a little difficult to handle as it requires time for you to brainstorm design ideas. Keep in mind that copyright issues are becoming more important than ever, so you can't just take any image from the internet to use for your messages.

Nevertheless, making sure you create appealing posts with allowable images should be a priority.

You will need to invest a significant amount of time in this process. This may pose a problem for most business owners who are already stretched in too many directions. But because the design is essential for engagement, there's no skipping or shortchanging this step.

A great way to make sure your designs are optimal for your campaigns is to use great templates. For example, at our Sold Out Houses Pro membership, we provide our members access to more than 1700+ different real estate marketing templates. (You can learn more about the membership at https://soldouthouses.com/vip)

They have created the ultimate collection of Instagram canvas templates that will ensure a truly diverse selection. When you have so many great templates at your disposal, you are never going to have to worry about searching for quality designs again.

10. Post Frequently

There is no better way to stand out from the competition in social media than to be more active than they are. But there is a downside to this if you don't do it right. Some business owners try to post every day, but they sacrifice quality which hurts more than helps their business.

The biggest concern when you sacrifice quality is your followers won't see you as a truly outstanding source of information. This could lead many of them to unfollow you and look for other sources of information that are more consistent with quality.

The key is to find the balance between quality and consistency, keeping in mind it's never good to sacrifice quality just to post frequently. This means if you can only produce one quality publication each week, it is better to do this than to post five times per week with rehashed and unoriginal content that your audience won't like.

11. Post at the Right Time

There is actual science to the process of posting your content on social media and achieving the highest engagement possible. You need to consider many factors to do this properly, like the target audience and their most common time to be online. There's also the best day of the week to post and concern for holidays and other events.

This type of calculation can mean the difference between a post seen by a handful of people versus one that is seen by hundreds or even thousands of people. Every single time you post something new, first consider what it will take to make the most impact.

12. Use Quality Hashtags

The use of hashtags is something that often confuses people when they are trying to use them for their post engagement. One of the main things to consider when this happens is that people are very likely to create hashtags without really considering the reasons why they will use them and how they will use them in their content.

13. Optimize Your Profile for Search

This is also a huge thing to consider because your profile is going to be the first thing most potential clients or customers see when they search for what they want. By having a truly attractive and engaging profile, you will increase your chances of being found by the people who want to buy what you are selling.

Optimizing your profile is not just about words but also about your choice of images, colors, and themes. There are many factors that will play a role in the appeal of your profile, so make sure that you take the time to do this the right way.

14. Interact with Your Followers

This is something you really need to work on because it will make a huge difference in the level of trust and loyalty you are able to create with your target audience.

It's always a good idea to use live streaming to show your face to your audience and have interactions with as many of them as possible.

When you do this, you create a sense of familiarity, and your audience can start to see you as a friend and not just someone who is trying to sell them something. This personalized engagement will play a huge role in your ability to retain your audience and boost conversions.

15. Diversify Your Content Type

One of the biggest mistakes people make on social media is that they only create a certain type of content. Some will post text with an image, others will stream online, and some will post audio clips.

The best approach to any social media promotional effort is to be diverse and to combine all types of media with your content.

The more you diversify your content type, the more it will maintain that fresh appeal with your audience. That said, the thing to keep in mind at all times is to maintain quality above everything else.

It's well-known that videos have grown in popularity on social media, but remember there's also power in a good post that contains text with an attractive image. Mix things up and keep your audience engaged with quality content, and the follower count will grow much faster.

16. Promote Your Social Media in Your Network

Sometimes one of the best ways to get a good initial boost with your social media efforts is to simply consider the use of your existing network of people to promote your page. This is going to be a great way to gain a bit of momentum as you start to create content.

It is easier to be able to see results when you are able to find a number of initial followers who can interact with your posts and share them with their network. This creates an immensely powerful snowball effect that can lead to a quick rise in your follower count.

17. Collaborate with Other Influencers

Collaborating with other influencers is always a great way for you to boost your presence and to start gaining more and more credibility in your realty niche. You should take the time to search influencers who have audiences that will find your services appealing.

Once you are able to collaborate with them, you could end up finding a huge audience that is going to follow your content as well. This is a great strategy for faster social media growth, and ultimately, we all want to be able to see a rise in our follower count as the most important goal.

18. Take Advantage of Special Events and Holidays

Make sure you take the time to prepare great content for specific holidays. As a realtor, this can be extremely useful when you are trying to engage your audience during a specific season or event.

Social Media Optimization

Approximately 2.77 BILLION people use social media worldwide. These people use their preferred social network in a number of ways. Some simply look to be entertained by it, while others use it for research and so on.

As a real estate agent trying to market to these people, you must ensure they find you when searching. Much like optimizing your website for search engines, you must optimize your profiles for social media.

How to Optimize Your Social Media Profile

You can optimize Facebook and Instagram in the same way. Each has a social profile you must complete. This is a requirement because it is how you will appear to users.

Before you write the information on the profile requests, you should do keyword research for social media. Yes, just like a website and doing keyword research for it, you need to do research for social networks.

Spend time searching the social network for what users are looking for on it. You can do this by typing some words into the search that pertain to your services. Remember, you are a real estate agent who wants people in your local area because if you market to people two states away from you, you won't gain any new clients. That's why when doing your research, filter the search for people in a certain city.

Look at the users that come up for the services you have searched for to make sure they are in the area of your office.

You can then look over their information and questions or comments they have made about certain services. Note certain attributes about them. For instance, you might take notes on:

- Age
- Questions
- Comments
- Male or Female
- Job/Career

Parent/Single/Married/Dating

These attributes will help you as you create content for your social media feed because you want it to pertain to the audience on the social network.

As you're searching for different services on the social network, pay attention to the ones that are brought up the most. Those are the ones you want to optimize your social media profile for when writing it.

Once you know the services people are discussing the most, you're ready to optimize your profile. There are certain keyword phrases you should always use as a real estate agent.

- Realtor in <city>
- Real estate agent in <city>
- <City> Realty office

This should be in your description. For example, "Mr. Dereck James is a realtor in New York City with 10 years of experience in the real estate industry."

The services you researched should be part of the description as well. To continue the description above, you can write something like: "Mr. Dereck James is a realtor in New York City with 10 years of experience in the real estate industry. He has helped more than 500 happy clients find their dream homes or sell their houses."

You have identified many of your services in your descriptions, and they are the ones that are most important to people on the social network for that description. When people search for any combination of those keyword phrases, your profile will show up because it's relevant to their search. Because of this, they will take notice of your services, post on your social media feed, and then click through to your website.

The Importance of Optimizing Your Social Media Profile Regularly

Optimizing your social media profile should be done regularly. Our recommendation is every two months. The reason for this is because people change what they search for, and you want to make sure your profile is current with what people care about at the time.

If you're unsure how to correctly optimize your social media profile, turn to the experts. We can help you optimize your social media profile to give you maximum visibility on social networks. When you have this, you can bring potential clients to your website to convert them to new clients.

Visit our site at https://soldouthouses.com to learn more about our products & services.

Social media is the first part of the S.W.I.F.T. method, and then you should turn your focus to your website.

WEBSITE

This is the second part in the S.W.I.F.T. method – your website. Your website is your virtual business card. It is the first page your potential prospects will see when they search for your services.

Now, you may wonder, "Why do I need a website if I already have a fan page?"

Indeed, with so many social media accounts out there, it seems there is no need for a website.

However, there are some potent powers a website has that can hardly be replaced by social media.

Before covering those features, let me share a story with you.

Before I started my first online business, I was a real estate agent.

I became a realtor because I wanted to learn one of the essential skills for business – selling.

But then, I was young and a novice. I knew nothing about marketing and selling. So all I did was give away flyers on the street or do cold calling and cold mailing, all the traditional stuff.

I worked 15 hours per day, but I still struggled to generate leads and get clients.

I started studying more about selling and real estate. I read books, took courses, and attended seminars.

I also created my first blog as my notebook. I wrote down everything I learned about buying a house, selling a house, or how to sign contracts. I included tips on the blog.

But having more knowledge does not help much. After a few months of feeling frustrated, I quit.

"I may never learn how to sell," I told myself, downcast.

One day, I got a phone call that changed my life.

"Hi, are you Nick?" The voice didn't sound familiar.

"Yes, who are you?" I asked

"I want you to help me sell my house!" the stranger replied.

I was puzzled since I was no longer an agent.

"How did you find me?" I asked

"It's your website. I found your website."

Then he explained how he found my website, read my blog material, and said that's why he wanted my help.

"I think you are a pro. I want to work with you," he explained.

After that, I started to get more and more phone calls every week asking if I could help them buy or sell houses.

I did some research and discovered my website was ranked on one of the local keywords.

That was the first time I realized the power of a website and SEO (search engine optimization).

Nowadays, I implement SEO in all my businesses and have built many profitable websites.

There are three primary reasons why having a website is essential and why social media cannot replace it.

1. **t gives you more control**
2. **It positions you as a leader in your industry**
3. **It brings you traffic from search engines.**

Social media content does not work well on Google. You leave many potential clients on the table if you only do social media marketing.

That is why you not only need to use social media, but also you need to have a website and implement Search Engine Optimization.

There are two major components of website optimization:

1. You must optimize it to convert more visitors to leads.
2. You must optimize it to get a higher ranking on Google.

So let's talk about how to design your website to bring more leads.

How to Design a Website to Generate More Leads

The way a website is designed matters to users. People must be able to find what they want and need in as little time as possible. The following are the layout and pages you need to have on your website to generate more leads.

Homepage

Your homepage should be simple but informative. State what you provide, where you are located, and how you are the best real estate agent in the area. A call-to-action should be placed through the page. You should also have a way for people to submit information so you can follow up with them, such as having a newsletter sign-up form.

Your homepage is the first impression people have of you, so it needs to be good.

Top Navigation

Besides the homepage content, the site should have top navigation. This top navigation should be set up like this:

- Home
- About Us
- Services
- Gallery
- Testimonials
- Contact Us

Link to these pages on the homepage as well.

About Us

This is the page on which you talk about yourself. You want to position yourself as an authority and a trust-worthy local expert in your area.

Be specific without making the descriptions too long. You want people to read the bios and information and leave the page feeling good about making an appointment with you. Be personable but professional.

Pictures are important for this page because it helps people connect with you and the practice. It brings them much closer to making an appointment. A video can be highly effective on this page, so consider making one with yourself and your team in it.

Services

You should have a page with a list of your realty services. Each service should have a description, and each one should link to a separate page for that service.

Also, the top navigation should have a drop-down menu that has each of those service pages. That way, people can find what they need right away.

The language should be clear and easy to understand. Do not use overly complicated terms to describe your real estate business.

People should be able to understand exactly what to expect when they leave the page.

Testimonials

People read reviews or testimonials to help them decide whether they want to buy a product or service. It's important to include a page like this on your site too.

All you need to do is place the testimonials on the page in an attractive way.

Then add or update the testimonials regularly to make them even more attractive to people who are still unsure if they want to make an appointment.

Contact Me

The contact page should be simple and informative. Provide a map, location information, and contact information.

A simple form for people to ask questions and book appointments is also a good idea.

Some real estate agents are adding the ability for prospects to book appointments right on the website. Consider this for your site, as people really prefer to do things quickly and easily. Plus, if you give them that opportunity, this could make it more likely they'll book an appointment.

Make Your Website Mobile Friendly

Most people use a mobile device to search the internet, especially when looking for a realtor. This means you have to ensure that your website is mobile-friendly. If you do not know how to transition your site to a mobile-friendly one, you may need a website developer to help. You can check if your website is mobile friendly at https://search.google.com/test/mobile-friendly

Once you have your website design established, it is time to add content to it. Content is incredibly important as well because it provides information to your users and clients. The following is how you can use content to position yourself and get more clients.

How to Optimize Your Website to Generate More Leads From Google

One of the biggest challenges businesses deal with in the modern world is the massive competition now flooding the offline and online markets.

The real estate industry is no different in this situation as more services are offered online and offline. This means that those who want to find new clients need to maximize the process of **Search Engine Optimization (SEO).**

The offline methods of advertising are becoming more and more obsolete as time passes. The digital world is now the ultimate place for any business to find customers. With that said, the competition likewise continues to grow larger and stronger.

What Is SEO Marketing in the Real Estate Industry?

Before we get into the specifics regarding SEO for the real estate industry, we need to understand what SEO means. It is essential to know what you have to do in order to achieve results.

Search engine optimization is the process of getting your website ranked higher on a search engine's search results. For example, when someone types a common search keyword like "realtor near me," you want to make sure your website is found on the first page.

The process of ranking your content on search engines like Google, Yahoo, or Bing is very complex. There are many factors and variables to consider. For example, your niche is going to play a major role in the kind of results you get.

When it comes to the real estate industry, there are different levels of competition. All of them depend on the size of the city where you have your realty office.

Regardless of how many competitors you are dealing with, it would help if you still considered those factors. One of these is the importance of a constant and reliable digital marketing strategy.

Why Do You Need to Do SEO?

The main purpose of search engine optimization is to increase the rank of your website on the Google search results page.

This is what your website needs. As a realtor, you can only enhance your business when you can consistently get new clients.

Search engine optimization is a great strategy to bring you consistent leads without spending money for ads on Google.

So if you want to build a long-term business, you should always consider using SEO as one of your major lead generation strategies.

What Are the Benefits of SEO to Real Estate Agents?

Here are some benefits of SEO to your real estate business. Have a look at them and start to invest in this marketing tool to achieve your goals.

1. Optimize Content

Content optimization is one of the ranking factors in the Google search algorithm. By using SEO, your content will get optimized, and this helps your website to come in the top spots.

In content optimization, SEO takes care of

- Images
- URL
- Meta Tags
- Header
- Title
- Content

For a good loading speed, all these things need to be optimized. Because without SEO optimization, your website will take many minutes to load, which can frustrate users.

2. Increase Online Visibility

SEO handles almost all the factors that help in ranking the website. It first focuses on the keywords. By using related location and brand keywords, you can help the users reach your page.

When people make a query on Google, it starts to search all the articles that contain those specific keywords. In this way, your website can come to the top places.

When people see your website, they will likely do a little research on you. With this, SEO also helps to add a brand on Google maps with directions so people can easily reach you.

3. Generate More Organic Traffic

With the help of related keywords, only those people will come to your website who have an interest in your services. SEO makes sure that your website is visible to only interested people. This helps save your money.

4. Increase Conversion Rate

SEO keeps the user interested in your website. When they are on the homepage, it automatically displays your best offers at affordable prices.

Clicking on these can redirect to the appointment page. If the users are interested in your services, then they will likely consider making an appointment.

How to Ensure the Best SEO Marketing Results

SEO can be a very overwhelming task to handle when you are unaware how it works. This proves to be very frustrating for many business owners who often lack experience with it.

The biggest problem when you have your own business is managing the many varied responsibilities. So much needs to get done, and we're all counting every minute that passes in a day. The modern world has turned into a very hectic, fast-paced race.

There are many important factors to keep in mind when creating your website. Some of them will take more time and experience than others, but they are all essential for the best results.

One of the most common mistakes people make is they overcomplicate the navigation on their website. If you browse a few random websites, you will notice that the navigation can range from extremely simple and intuitive to confusing and frustrating.

It is important that all of the relevant links on your website are easy to access. This, in turn, will make it easier for you to achieve the results you want and need.

A website must be optimized to perform well on a search engine. Understanding how a search engine works will help you understand the importance of website optimization and how to do it properly.

How Search Engines Work

When someone goes to a search engine like Google, the person types in a few words that relate to what they are looking for at that moment. For instance, they may type in "realtors in NYC." When they hit enter, Google will show them websites belonging to realtors in NYC. How does Google know those websites belong to realtors in NYC? Those websites are optimized.

When a website's information pertains to "realtors in NYC," Google knows that people will be interested in it. This means all those realtors have to do for their website is add-in "realtors in <their city>," right? Not exactly.

How Does Google Decide to Rank Content?

SEO is like a balancing act. You need to make sure you are working on the aspects that the search engine finds most relevant and important. There are several factors to consider, which include the following:

- The content on your website pages
- The proper use of popular keywords
- The length and quality of your blog content
- The loading times for your website
- A mobile-friendly structure
- The time visitors spend on your website
- The inbound links or backlinks to your site

Now, let's review these aspects in more detail to help you understand the importance of each one.

#1. The Content on Your Website Pages

This is different from the content on your blogs or social media. It is meant to give people the most essential and valuable information regarding your business. This is about your mission, vision, services, and credentials as a real estate agent.

The information must be written concisely, to the point. The idea is to help people find out as much as they need about your services without reading a long page of text.

Do not allow any of the content on your website to be filler. This means avoiding any content that is not valuable and useful.

#2. The Proper Use of Popular Keywords

Keywords play an exceptionally important role in your ability to climb the ranks. Think about proper keyword use as the link between your content and the search engines.

This means that the focus of your SEO efforts needs to be on optimizing the keywords you are using. The real estate niche offers a variety of keywords that have different levels of popularity.

It's always a dynamic process to choose the right keywords. The term "dynamic" here refers to possible changes based on several factors. Some keywords remain the same at all times; certain long-tail keywords will change.

#3. The Length and Quality of Your Blog Content

Writing blogs and articles for a website is going to be crucial for SEO success.

If you want your website to rank higher on search engines, you need to be constantly creating material that is both informative and original. This means avoiding plagiarism at all costs.

It is a good idea to use tools like Copyscape to check your content. This tool scans the web to see if your material exists anywhere else.

It is important to note that Google can penalize any website that uses existing content, which is terrible for organic growth.

This is a delicate situation that could harm your business for a long time. That is why you have to make sure you don't waste time with rehashed and copied material. It does more harm than good in the to your business.

#4. The Loading Times for Your Website

Some people work hard on their website content but fail to see the importance of ensuring it has optimal loading times. The modern digital consumer is very impatient, and the average time they spend on a website often depends on how fast it's loading.

#5. A Mobile-Friendly Structure

The need for mobile-friendly structures on websites has been an important part of web design for several years now, but it is still worth mentioning here. The main reason is to call out the surprising number of websites that still use a static design which is not mobile-friendly.

Keep in mind that Google has been vocal about its preference for mobile-friendly websites for both their mobile search engine results and their standard search engine results.

This means that people browsing the web from their mobiles will always see mobile-friendly websites in their results, but the same will happen with visitors who use desktops and laptops to browse the web.

#6. The Time Visitors Spend on Your Website

This is also a big factor search engines consider when they rank your website. But perhaps you're getting too many bounce visitors, those who only spend a few seconds or less than a minute.

The bounce rate is the percentage of people who are leaving the site too fast. This is a clear indicator they are not staying long enough to read the content. All that material that's available to them isn't seen for whatever reason.

Improving the time your visitors spend on your site is always going to be worthwhile.

#7. The Inbound Links or Backlinks to Your Website

Backlinks are otherwise known as inbound links, one-way links, and incoming links. These are the links from one site to another site or a page.

Major search engines and Google consider backlinks votes for specific pages. The more high-quality links you get, the higher your site ranks on Google or other engines.

You cannot consider all backlines equal, as they are of various types. To gain a higher rank on Google's search results page, you need to focus on quality backlinks.

In simple terms, 1,000 low-quality backlinks will do no good, but a single backlink with high-quality will. So those with quality backlinks share the same traits as other such backlinks. A link from https://cnn.com can have 10,000 times more ranking power than a link from a newly created website.

Backlinks are important because they provide the authenticity of a website to the search engine crawlers. The better the network you build through backlinks, the better the chance you will have to gain a higher ranking in the search engine results.

The Importance of Keyword Research

When you optimize your website, you need to conduct keyword research. This means to research keyword phrases that people are using on the search engine.

You can use Google's Keyword Planner or a third party such as Keyword.io. You only need to enter words that concern your realty office and its services to see what people have been searching on Google. The results will show you exact keyword phrases, volume (how often the keyword phrase was searched), and competition.

When selecting keyword phrases, look for these factors:

1. Relevance

Does the keyword phrase pertain to what you offer your prospects? If so, it may be good for your website.

2. Volume

Do many people search for that keyword phrase? If so, it also may be a good fit for your website.

3. Competition

Do a lot of other sites try to rank for it on Google? If not, use it on your site.

When you start optimizing your website, choose keyword phrases that are relevant, have high volume, and have low competition. As you gain traffic and trust with Google, you can optimize for more competitive keyword phrases. It takes time to strengthen your website to the point Google will rank you for more competitive keyword phrases, but it is possible with time and effort.

How to Optimize Your Site with Keyword Phrases

Once you have the list of keyword phrases you're ready to optimize your site. You want to use them in four areas.

Content

Place the keyword phrase naturally into the content two or three times if it's about 500 words. Use them more for longer material.

Headers

The keyword phrases should be used in at least one sub-header.

Title Tag

The title tag is the page title displayed on Google's search results pages. Use the keyword phrase in this title because people are more likely to click on your website if they see the keyword phrase they searched for.

Meta Description

The meta description is the description under the title tag in Google's search results pages. Also, use the keyword phrase in it to further encourage people to click on your website listing.

You should have at least one image on the page with an ALT tag that includes the keyword phrase.

Once you've included the keyword phrase in these four locations of the website (in addition to the image), you've optimized the page successfully.

Optimizing Additional Pages

Each page of your site should be optimized for a keyword phrase. When you've optimized each page of the site, start producing more content to increase the number of pages in Google's index. The more pages you have, the more chances of bringing traffic to your site.

That said, while you could continue to create pages on your site, it's a better idea to create a blog instead. This is where you can add information about your services.

The pages of your site should simply be information about you, any other realtors, the realty office, a page for each service, a contact page, and then the blog page. Under the blog page, you will have posts. Each post can be indexed in Google.

You can optimize each post as you do the pages. Use a relevant keyword phrase for the post. Add it to the content, a subheader, title tag and meta description. You should also have an image that has an optimized alt tag.

Add Content Regularly to Increase Traffic

The more content you add to your site, the more traffic you will receive. Think about all the people using the internet.

If you can meet their needs with your information, they will be much more likely to seek your services. Since it's hard to meet everyone's needs at once, you have to continue adding content.

As you add to your blog, you will soon see it is bringing more traffic to your site.

Continue to do keyword research every month. You will find that keyword phrases change over time because people naturally change the way they ask questions or seek services.

Updating your site to coincide with what people are searching for and how they are searching for it will ensure you continue to get in front of people looking for your services before your competition does.

Get Started and Do Not Stop

Now is the time to optimize your website. As we've discussed, start with keyword research. Use those keyword phrases to optimize each page of the site. Write blog posts optimized with other keyword phrases. You can then go back to researching keyword phrases to use more of them in posts.

Steps to Rank Your Website Better

Over fifty percent of consumers use a search engine to find a real estate agent in their local area. If real estate agents don't optimize their websites, those people will never find them. That equates to thousands of dollars lost in appointments.

An agent's website is the most important part of digital marketing. It's the hub for information. Making sure the site is optimized in the right way will ensure people not only find you but also book an appointment.

Understanding how to optimize and promote a website online for maximum visibility is important. It is what can make a real estate agent successful.

Tips for Successful Search Engine Optimization

The following search engine optimization (SEO) tips can increase your online presence.

#1: Claim Your Google My Business Listing

Google My Business was designed by Google to provide its users with information about local businesses, including realty offices. You must claim your listing if you want to show up in local search results. When someone in your local area searches for "realtors near me," the only way you will show up is if you have Google My Business.

Once you claim your Google My Business listing, you should also complete the profile. The more information you provide, the better. Google favors businesses that use Google My Business to serve their consumers.

Managing a Google My Business listing means adding new photos and posts to it weekly. This is what will help you climb the local search engine rankings.

#2: Optimize with Local Keywords

Your site should be optimized with the keyword that people in your local area use when looking for real estate agents. Google's Keyword Planner is a great tool to see what consumers are typing in when looking for a realtor.

Be as specific as possible when trying to rank for keyword phrases because general ones rarely get ranked. Use smaller cities and neighborhoods besides where you are located to bring in people who may search for those areas with keyword phrases such as "realtor near Spring."

#3: Encourage Reviews

Reviews are crucial these days. Eighty-four percent of people trust online reviews more than they trust what their friends tell them. Sixty-eight percent of people decide about a business after reading one to six reviews online.

The best way to encourage reviews is to remind clients on their way out of the office that you're on Facebook and Google, so their reviews would be appreciated. You can follow up that request with an email thanking them for coming in for the appointment and, once again, asking for a review.

#4: Provide Valuable Information on Your Website

Your website should have a library of material on it to interest people before and after their appointments. It should include information about buying a house, selling a house, real estate industry news, and all kinds of local information.

The site also needs to encourage users to contact the agent for an appointment. The most effective way is to present the problems people have, the risks of not doing something about them, the solutions available, and then what to do to get those solutions.

The website should have several pages (one for each service, an about page, a contact page, and a blog). Landing pages should be created for each campaign, and the blog should be added to regularly.

#5: Use Social Media

Social media doesn't have a direct influence on website rankings, but it does indirectly affect it. Promoting your site on social media will bring people to your site. As more people visit from social media, the more Google will take notice, and the algorithm will be more likely to rank your site for the keyword phrases you're using to optimize it.

Set up social networks like Facebook, Twitter, Instagram, Pinterest, and/or LinkedIn. Once you have those set up, be sure to remain active on them. This includes posting photos from inside of the office and sharing links with valuable information. The more you use the social network, the bigger your following will be, which will bring you new leads.

#6: Update Website as Needed

The internet is changing nearly every day so you must make sure your website stays up to date. Right now, it should be mobile-friendly because as much as 70 percent of searches are performed on a mobile device. The website should be at an optimal speed because people are typically impatient and won't wait for a website to load.

As we move ahead, websites will need other changes, and it's important to stay current as they are released.

#7: Build Citations

Citations are listings in online directories. Usually, these listings only include Name, Address and Phone Number (NAP). There are hundreds of online directories to submit your information to, and it should be done over time instead of using a tool to do it.

The more citations you build for your realty office, the more Google will trust you. The Google bots note the information in those listings and make sure it's the same exact information on your website.

This also means you must have your Name, Address and Phone Number on every page of your site. The easiest way to do that is to put it in the footer.

#8: Building Backlinks

Backlinks are one of the most essential parts of Search Engine Optimization. Those are links from other websites to your website. Search engines use backlinks as a ranking signal. The more high-quality backlinks you get, the better the chance you will have to gain a higher ranking in the search engine results.

Link building is a process of creating authoritative links for your website and attracting more traffic to your website for your content. It requires efficient backlinking techniques that compel the users to click on the links and come to your website. My team can help you with both content optimization and link building. If you are interested, contact us at **https://soldouthouses.com**

SEO Marketing Takes Time, Knowledge, and Effort

There is one problem many business owners have with SEO regarding their perception of the amount of work required to succeed with their business.

Some expect to see amazing results by uploading a few articles sporadically. The truth is SEO requires much more than just creating quality material now and then.

One way to understand this is to consider the massive number of competitors in any given niche. For example, there are only 8 to 10 available spots on the first page of any Google search result. This means there will be just 10 websites who get those spots out of potentially hundreds of thousands of websites.

With that said, not all websites in a niche are going to be active enough to even compete for a spot on the first page results. It's important to also note that the Google algorithm is going to accommodate different websites at any given moment during a search so that hundreds of different websites can rotate and become part of those search results.

The only way any website can land on the first page on Google is to be consistent with every SEO effort. The good news is there are ways to lower the saturation of competitors in any given niche.

For example, a SEO marketing expert can search keywords that are less popular but still strong enough to bring in hundreds of leads to you.

This requires a very intricate strategy that requires the use of different levels of keyword popularity to see what kind of results are possible. Not only that, but you also have to ensure all of the content that is uploaded to your site is both original and engaging.

With that said, many variables must be considered. Those variables go beyond content and also beyond your niche. Only those who are experts in the world of SEO could help you effectively handle those variables.

How to Get Help with SEO

SEO is not easy, especially when you're running a successful business. You not only need to add content and be active on social media, but you must fix any website problems that arise and also update as needed. All this work is best performed by a professional.

We are a digital marketing agency that specializes in SEO for real estate agents and companies. We use a proven and effective marketing strategy called S.W.I.F.T., which stands for social media, website, information, funnel, and traffic. By implementing the latest SEO best practices and incorporating social media, we can bring quality traffic to your site that converts into new clients for your real estate business.

Contact Us for Help with Website Optimization

Website optimization is a necessity for success with online marketing. It's why it's the second part of our S.W.I.F.T. method. If you need help with optimizing your website, turn to the experts. We can do it quickly and correctly so you can bring in new leads sooner. You can go to **https://soldouthouses.com** for more information.

You can also sign up for my free real estate marketing checklist at **https://soldouthouses.com/checklist** to learn more about real estate marketing.

INFORMATION

How to Use Content to Position Yourself and Get More Clients

Information is the next step in the S.W.I.F.T. method. Information here means content. It is what will convince people to come to your website, which is how you will feed your funnel.

The internet is made up of content. Every single facet of it is content. When you read an article, it is content. When you watch a video, it is content. When you see an image, it is content. It is all content, and it's what people want from the internet and you.

I discovered the power of content very early. When I first started my business, I had a miniscule budget for advertising.

I was struggling to get more website visitors, and I needed to find a way to promote my business.

I jumped on Facebook groups, forums, and Yahoo Answers to seek help. I got a lot of replies. And not surprising, many of them were nothing but spam.

However, I found a guy from Singapore who answered all my questions professionally. He posted professional content related to my marketing questions. I started to follow him and added him as a Facebook friend.

Then within a few days, I became his customer and bought his course.

His course wasn't really impressive, but I realized what he was doing to promote his business. He answered my questions with valuable content and led me to his website.

I decided to give this strategy a try.

I went to Yahoo Answers to answer questions. Within a few days, I got my first customers, and Yahoo Answers marketing became one of my core marketing strategies to get clients.

That was the first time I realized the power of content.

A few years later, Yahoo restricted the usage of the links and became less effective. So I started implementing different kinds of publishing strategies to get clients.

- Blogging
- YouTube
- Podcasts
- eBooks

Even today, content marketing is still one of my best marketing strategies to bring in new clients on a regular basis.

Content Is King

One of the most important things to understand about digital marketing is that content continues to be the most powerful way to achieve results.

You can always invest in Google ads if you want to see fast results, but if you want longevity and if you want to build authority, you need to make sure that you have great content to obtain organic reach.

This means you need to be very consistent with the content that you create, and you have to ensure it's highly valuable to the readers.

Do not forget that every single day you do not publish something new, there is a good chance your competitors are creating content that will rank higher. Real estate is not a massively saturated niche, but most geographic areas likely have several dozen real estate agents who are competing for a good spot on the local search results.

Many formulas are used for SEO. Some of them are overly complex, and others are more simplistic. But they all revolve around the importance of content. If the content you produce is great, you are going to start to see a better organic reach as your content is ranked higher.

One of the best things about content creation is that it can help your website land a spot on the first page on Google with a specific set of keywords. This is one of the reasons it is a good idea to think of new publications on your website as an opportunity to rank your content higher on the results.

You could have no content on the first page at one point, but a single new post could turn the tides and reach the first page results. This alone could translate to massive exposure for a set amount of time.

What Type of Content Can You Publish?

There are many ways to produce content and ways to use it. The following are a few that can deliver information on social media and your website.

Articles

Articles deliver information, of course. People search for answers to their questions all the time. When they see articles from a realtor, such as yourself, that answer their questions, they will appreciate it. If they notice you're in their area, they will be more likely to contact you for an appointment if that's what they need.

The quality of articles matters. You must thoroughly answer questions the readers have. Providing details about the topic will help them feel as though they are getting exactly what they need in order to make a decision about a concern at that moment. People form an impression of the author of an article, too, so make it a good one.

People obviously need to understand the articles as well. It's important to use non-technical terms when writing for potential clients. Pretend you're speaking to them directly. This will help you write in a way people can relate to.

Articles don't always have to be about answering questions though. They can also provide information to internet users. Helping them improve their lives can leave a great impression. Writing about tips for finding a dream home or selling a house quickly (and for more money) can really draw people in. This can be the first step in turning them into new clients.

These articles can be placed on your site, and then you can take the link and promote it on Facebook and Instagram. Use an attractive image with it to spark people's attention.

Images

Images are another type of content real estate agents should use to gain the attention of new clients. These images should always be of high quality and relevant. Here are a few types of images realtors can use to draw people to their websites.

Images of Properties You Are Selling

A picture is worth a thousand words. Posting high-quality images of the properties you are selling can easily catch your ideal prospect's attention.

Infographic

Infographics are powerful tools to convey your idea. Sometimes people don't like reading on social media. With an infographic, you can easily convey your ideas.

Buyer & Seller Tips

Sharing tips about buying and selling houses positions you as the expert in both your local area and your industry. This type of content makes your audience trust and like you more.

Real Estate Terms

There are many terms in the real estate industry, and it can be daunting for your audience to learn about them. Posting images that explain those terms can help you communicate with your clients better.

Quotes

Quotes go viral easily. People like to share quotes from authorities or celebrities. Sharing images of quotes can easily bring you viral traffic from social media.

FAQ

Your ideal clients have many questions, and you can answer them with your posts. Sharing that type of content not only helps your audience have better clarity about real estate, it also shows your prospects how much you care about them.

You can upload images everywhere. Place them on your website on a gallery page, on your blog posts, and then on social media, such as Facebook and Instagram. These images will get a lot of attention if they provide value to your followers.

If you are too busy to create your own image posts, our Sold Out Houses Pro membership gives you tons of done-for-you content and social media templates for you to plug-and-play to your business. You can go to https://soldouthouses.com/vip to sign up for a 14-day free trial.

Videos

Videos are another type of content that many real estate agents could use more often. Start creating different types of videos to get the word out about you, your realty office, and your services.

Informative Videos

Sharing valuable information can easily position you as the local expert, and people love working with experts. That's why offering valuable content is always a great way to market yourself.

Testimonials

People love to watch others talk about their experience with a particular realtor. While reviews are good to have, videos can be much better. They show how real the review is, and people connect with it much more.

Videos of the House You Are Selling

With the help of technology, you can now sell houses with videos. You can introduce the house you are selling and show the benefits and features of it. And it may bring you some sales and leads without delivering open houses.

50 Most Engaging Content Types to Publish on Social Media

Great content can not only bring you more website visitors from search engines, but it can also bring more potential clients from social media.

As the world has evolved, social media has become a component of the marketing strategy for almost every brand. But even an expert marketer can fall into despair if pressed to create an original design for a social media campaign within a deadline.

To inspire you and generate ideas, I want to share in this next section the 50 most engaging and viral content types to post on your social media and website.

1. Infographics

Infographics can be an effective way to convey a ton of information about your company, brand, or product using visuals. They have the ability to turn boring statistics into eye-catching details and keep your audience hooked.

Whether it's your infographic or a masterpiece from a curator, a classy infographic can draw viewers to your social media post and keep them engaged.

You can also get my done-for-you real estate infographic package at https://soldouthouses.com/infographics

2. Motivational Posts

All people go through challenges in life, and what can lighten the mood is a little motivation. When targeted to the right audience at the right time, a motivational post can generate a lot of interest in your social media account.

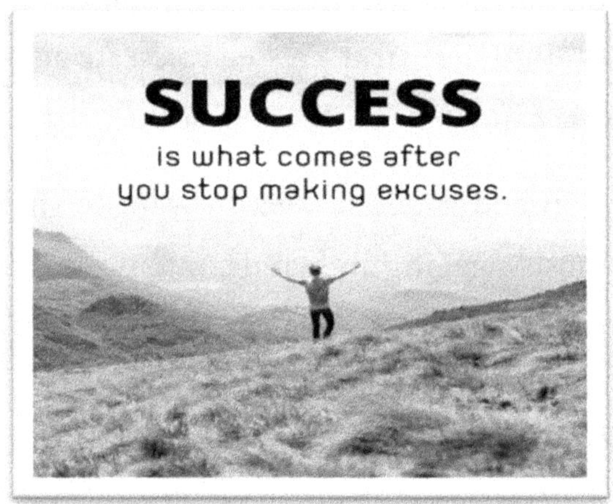

These motivational posts can be designed by referring to currently trending topics, but what will make your motivational post stand out from the rest is using carefully chosen words to build people up.

3. Long Articles

The term long articles here refers to inspirational stories or the experiences of celebrities or influencers who share their life experiences and day-to-day struggles.

These types of uplifting and educational articles about overcoming difficulty can steer a wide range of traffic towards your post and bring in leads and followers.

4. Plan Cohesive Campaigns

Building a complete campaign can be an effective way to drive a message home. Many people struggle to maintain their social media posts and get used to generating one-off posts just to keep up. Or they write a post on the fly to meet a deadline.

But building up an intentional, complete campaign will help you stay organized. And it's more likely to generate enough traffic to bring sustained results.

The campaigns can be either a series of posts to promote your product or a chain of branded posts that carries a consistent hashtag or a message.

5. The Blog Post of Your Website

Does your business website contain a blog? If so, social media is a great place to steer traffic to your blog.

Sharing your company's blog on your social media platform can be fruitful content for your social media account while giving your blog publicity too.

6. Posts Showing Your Happy Clients

There's hardly a better way to showcase your business than by sharing a post that shows the value you bring to clients.

Whenever you help a client find their dream home or sell a house, you should post their stories on social media, letting your audience know your value as a realtor.

7. Industry News

When it comes to the popularity of articles, the ones that share current news tend to attract more traffic and hence get more shares than an article on some mundane topic.

If you share the latest gossip or a tidbit about ongoing operations in your niche, then you're more likely to attract leads to your social media platform.

Creating industry news doesn't have to be complicated. Just convert a recent development in your surroundings into a post and tweet about it.

8. Curated Content

Curated content is one of the simplest ways to create a post for your social media platform. The term curated content simply means to share the content of other people within your niche. Sometimes the post you want to share with your audience is already designed or written by other people.

Rather than converting or creating a post of your own, you can simply share their post and give them credit. The advantage of curated content is you don't need to create your own, and your social media stays updated simultaneously.

9. Question Posts

Everything you share on social media doesn't have to be in the form of information or articles. Sometimes you need to seek feedback from your people since it's the thoughts and opinions of customers that make your company grow.

A question as simple as, "What sort of content should I blog about next?" is enough to generate engagement in your post.

10. Posting Videos or Photos of Your Company

Visuals make your social media classy and eye-catching. Research shows that videos in particular bring a greater organic reach. So keep posting those photos, but now and then post videos of your company or product to grab the attention of viewers.

11. Customer Reviews and Testimonials

Every company or product has some dedicated fans. Let the voices of your fans be heard since they make your product better with their reviews and feedback.

You can design a comment or response for your valuable customers and thank them for believing in your company.

Sharing customer reviews will not only create amazing content for your social media account but also mentioning your customers in your posts will be appreciated by them.

12. Quick Tips and Advice

Most everyone is searching for tips and tricks to help with daily life. So besides sharing articles about the realty business, you can pique interest by posting helpful tips on topics you think will interest your clients.

You can also get 365 days of done-for-you social media content at https://soldouthouses.com/365doneforyoucontent

13. Memes or GIFs

When it fits, incorporating entertainment can liven up an article. Memes or GIFs work for this and grab the audience's attention. You can share information about your company or your product with humor.

Besides being the language of the modern audience, memes and GIFs also receive far more likes, shares, and retweets than an average social media post. They add a fun spin to your plain and dry posts and make it irresistible for your audience to skip through to the end.

You'll want to make sure the meme and GIF relate to your business.

14. Contest Posts

Many people love to participate in contests, especially when there's a giveaway.

The giveaway can be a small gift card, a free service, a product from your company, or a novelty, something creative that will interest people. The point is the contest generates attention from viewers and urges them to participate. Contest posts can be some of the best draws to more followers.

Just be clear about the objective of the contest and brainstorm ways to get your audience to participate.

15. Holiday Posts

No matter how successful a business you run or how in-demand your product is, you need to post content on social media that gives people an idea of how you relieve stress.

And what could be more attention-grabbing than posting some aesthetic pictures of a holiday destination that the employees or boss are planning to go on?

With these posts, you're sure to generate engagement. And your audience will love the fact that the employees of your company are real people who love to take their days off to enjoy their lives.

16. Photos from Company Events

You may be familiar with our cultural post idea and want to go a step beyond that. This could be a viable pick. Think of a couple of events your company has organized or participated in over the years.

Take the pictures of that function and post them on your social media account with the caption "Flashback." Not only will this educate people about your company's past, but it will also allow employees to relive that splendid day.

If this is not possible, if you were involved in a charity event or fundraiser, your social media would be a great place to spread awareness of the organization.

17. Post an Answer to a Commonly Asked Question

You must have received tons of emails or direct messages on your social media platform where customers ask different questions. Instead of solving the user queries one by one, you can create a social media post that contains the answer to one of the common questions to solve it once and for all.

You may want to make sure your answer is broad and detailed so it covers issues of those who asked similar questions. Handling the customers' concerns in this way can have a positive impact and keep readers engaged.

18. Start a Conversation with a Leader in Your Industry

Nowadays, people who are in high positions in their firms are coming on social media to crosstalk with a fellow employee and discuss the operations and proceedings of the company.

Cross-promoting by having a conversation with someone within your niche can be a good way to spread awareness and information about your company and product and hence attract potential leads to your social media account.

19. Links to Free Resources

Everyone loves to get free stuff, whether it's ebooks or white papers. So the audience is sure to appreciate the free resources you offer about the real estate business.

Create a link that provides users with access to an ultimate bundle or a downloadable infographic that shows them about the industry and provides helpful information.

Share and promote this link on your social media account, thereby increasing your reach with those seeking services like yours.

20. Podcast Episodes

If you want to run your social media successfully and give tough competition to other developing brands, then you need to think of something beyond just publishing articles.

Reading tons of information is no fun! Apart from being time-consuming, it can make your viewers super bored. One solution to grab their attention is to start your own podcast and publish it on your social media account.

Podcasts not only give the audience's eyes a break, but they also attract potential leads.

21. New Job Listings

Are you looking forward to expanding your team? Then how about choosing your next new employee from your audience.

Someone who's been one of your company's fans and witnessed the growth over time is likely to be hardworking and dedicated.

When posting a job listing on your social media account, give a good description of the position and duties.

22. Hiring Announcements and New Team Members

Once you post your job listings on your social media account, you'll probably get the right candidate in no time. Now, take it a step further and create a post to introduce the person to your audience.

In your post, you can share the person's qualifications, hobbies, and what they're looking forward to at work in your business. Welcoming a new team member is likely to grab the interest of potential leads.

23. "On This Day in History" Posts

Research or think of something that happened a year back (or longer) on an exact date, and let your users know about it. You can have fun with this post by choosing a happy day from your past, personally or professionally, or something unrelated to you but interesting.

24. Event Promotion

Social media is a great place to let your audience know of an event you have coming up, whether it's big or small. You can make a show of it by creating banners, interesting logos, and using trending hashtags. This not only boosts interest in the event, it also lets your audience know more about you, your business, and what you're up to.

25. Live Videos

If you have been using social media for a while, you know most apps like Instagram, Facebook, Snapchat, etc., provide the opportunity to interact with followers and fans by going live from your social media account.

Before going live, however, consider what platform will have the most appeal so enough viewers will be interested in watching it. Often people aren't available at a fixed time and therefore can't interact with you.

Once the live video is complete, post it on your social media account. It's great content on your account, and people who couldn't attend can watch the video and make comments.

26. Promote Email Sign-Ups

If your company is organizing a webinar or demo to educate or brief viewers on a particular topic, you'll need to let your audience know about it. You can post sign-up forms for these events, making sure that the invitation is detailed and eye-catching.

A post like this can generate leads as well as make your webinar a success.

27. Image Scrambles

To be clear, the term "image scrambles" means an image that is hard to read by an audience.

Many well-known brands post scrambled images on their social media accounts when they launch a new product and allow people to guess what the scrambled image means.

Viewers love to figure out what's going on. You could do this with an image, too, to get people involved with your post.

28. Inspirational Quotes

Many social media marketers find inspirational quotes to be cheesy and avoid them. But if used correctly, it's an effective way to reach your audience and keep them interested in your social media.

Your audience would love to be motivated and inspired by a short message from someone famous, a leader in your company, or even you. It's an easy way to make a quick connection and keep things simple and fresh for your followers.

29. Company Accomplishments

Whether you agree with this or not, your fans and audience care about you and want you to succeed in every aspect of your life.

So share your achievements and successes with your viewers. Let them in on every victory you have.

Whether it's selling a house or receiving an award for a decade of service at work or something else, let them know. Include your audience in your happiness!

30. Host a Twitter Chat

One way to connect with your audience and bring in loads of potential leads is to host a Twitter chat.

Hosting a Twitter chat means inviting your fans and audience to have a conversation. They share their thoughts and reviews over one unique hashtag. You can promote this new initiative on your social media so people can participate.

31. Social Media Polls

With polls you are prioritizing what your audience wants to see on your account. They always have expectations from you, and what better way to satisfy them than by tuning your next post to their suggestions and advice.

It could be as simple as posting a question, "What do you think our next post should be?" This way you've made them participants in the content and encouraged them to share their thoughts in the comment section. And increasing involvement usually means increasing leads.

32. How-to Videos

Besides going live or posting lengthy paragraphs to explain the functionality of your products or services, videos are an easy way to get your point across.

Often a short how-to video is perfect for showing rather than telling what needs to be done. Maybe it's navigating something on your website or the internet or tending to some task your viewers need to buy or sell a home. Whatever it is, your audience will appreciate the clarity of a how-to video.

33. Client Reviews

Reviews play an essential role in the life of the audience. Whenever they need to purchase something, they'll likely look at the product reviews. Since reviews are also proven to be the sales driver of your services, they are important content on your social media account.

34. Images or Videos of the Houses You Are Selling

There's a famous saying attributed to a nobleman that goes, "The most attractive product sells the best." That's certainly true in real estate. You can grab your viewers' attention and generate engagement by having beautiful pictures of the houses you're selling arranged attractively on your social media.

35. Question/Answer Session

Hosting a question-answer session on your social media platform can be fruitful as it enables your audience to ask and clarify issues that are important to them.

A question-answer session can help your articles, videos, and other material be directed toward topics that appeal to your viewers. And that can increase their engagement.

36. Spotify Playlists

Do your friends admire your taste in music? Sharing music with friends is one of the best ways to discover new artists and new bands.

Sharing music is also a great way to connect with someone, giving you a purpose in speaking to them. You can learn a lot about someone when you start talking about music!

Spotify has tools that allow you to share your personalized playlists. Some of your audience might really love knowing what you're listening to!

37. User-Generated Content

If you have amazing fans, then it's only fair you share fan-worthy content with them as well!

A lot of actors and influencers give "shout-outs" to the fans who do something related to their celebrity or leave amazing product reviews. An example of this is when a fan posts a photo of themself with gear from a brand. To be honest, it feels like a huge win when this happens!

38. Posts Telling about the Company's History

If you have been the one whose brand or company has been around for quite some time, then you have a lot of history to share with fans so they'll trust you!

When people see a business progress from where it started to where it currently is, they'll feel motivated and inspired by your brand.

Sharing your history is a great way to continue building your reputation and keeping your fans intrigued.

39. Company Announcements

Sharing news with your fans can make them feel like they are a part of your company. And it's also a great way to generate leads! Is your business moving, expanding, adding new services?

What better way of generating interest than sharing the news publicly! Let the people who care about you get excited too.

40. Create a Regular Series

Are you still uninspired? Still searching for ways to create unrealistic leads? This could be an option for you: to create a weekly series or a show. There are two ways to do this:

- Using the standard talk show format
- Bringing in a star guest each week

There are businesses such as Paste that are benefiting from this strategy.

41. Repurpose Blog Graphics

Designing new visual content for every individual social media post can be time and resource-consuming. Innovate a bit and use blog graphics with social media in mind!

If you decide to do this, you need to create versions of your blog graphics accurately for the platform you are going to be using. You can even create whole campaigns using blog graphics!

42. Share How-to Videos

We mentioned making a how-to video. But you can also share one that already exists. The internet is known for helping people make sense of something. By doing this, you project a positive image of your brand and yourself. After all, you are saving someone the time of searching for the information themself.

If you also happen to be selling a product that requires a how-to video, posting that could help buyers as well.

43. Case Studies:

People love seeing and hearing a positive review. Do you have a client who has nothing but positive things to say about you?

You can get that client in on a case study that you are doing and then share it with your followers on social media!

44. Share a Survey

Surveys are a good way to learn about your customers and get their feedback on many things. This will allow you to build stronger leads and see how to better promote your business.

As a bonus, it will also make your followers feel special.

45. Promote a New Event

A good way to build excitement is to give your audience the inside scoop on something that will be launched shortly or some event the company plans to arrange.

This will make them feel like they are part of the closed-loop and will allow you to gain more leads and followers.

46. Share a Fill-in-the-Blank Post

As already mentioned, making your audience feel like their opinions are valued can make it easier to generate leads and attract more clients.

If you are looking for ways to hear something from your fans, then a Fill-in-the-Blank post is a good option! This will allow you to hear the unique reviews and opinions of your customers.

47. Reshare Your Top Performing Posts

Doing something unique is not always the answer. One of the ways to generate leads via social media is to share your greatest hits!

This will turn a lot of online followers into buyers thereby bringing you profits! After all, everyone loves positive solutions.

48. Share Some Interesting Industry Research

In today's world, having up-to-date information and research is an important factor in staying ahead of your competition. One way you could keep your followers intrigued and generate more leads is by sharing statistics that are related to your field!

But don't stop there. Use these statistics to explain how your service or product is valuable, that is how something can be improved with the services you offer. Make sure the statistics you provide are accurate.

49. Preview a New Product or Event

One way for your fans and followers to love you more is to highlight upcoming products or events in your industry before they're common knowledge. After all, everyone loves being looped into something unknown to the general public.

You can get a lot of new followers and clients by regularly sharing snippets that sound like breaking news. This will allow you to get more leads since followers will want to check in to see what's new.

50. Giveaways!

Who doesn't like freebies? One way to generate active leads and gain more clients is by offering something free.

This will enhance your brand's recognition and allow you to build a better reputation. Start brainstorming for giveaways big or small you think will be an incentive for your audience.

We see this all the time. For instance, at one point Sony was offering a free customized theme for a PlayStation when customers pre-ordered a game.

Create Content and Promote It

The best way to attract new clients is to create content and promote it on your website and social media. You have something valuable to share with people, and that is what will drive them to you.

This is the next part of our S.W.I.F.T. method – funnel. You have the information portion with the content, so now you just need to funnel people.

Need Help with Content Creation?

Creating content can be a hassle for most real estate agents. The good news is my team has a solution. You can join our Sold Out Houses Pro Membership to get access to all kinds of done-for-you content as well as other real estate marketing tools. You can sign up for a 14-day free trial at https://soldouthouses.com/vip .

FUNNEL

So far, we have covered social media, website, and information. Now, it's time to put everything together.

I am going to introduce you to the idea of a marketing funnel.

But first, I want to share a story with you.

Six years ago, I started selling on Amazon. I sourced products from Alibaba, shipped them to Amazon's warehouse, did some keyword optimization, and bought Amazon ads. Within a few weeks, sales started coming in. And it was profitable. I was excited and thought, "That's it! I found a way to make money online. I should be able to retire early."

I became arrogant, overconfident and told myself, "If I can sell my product successfully on Amazon, I should be able to make money on Facebook as well." So I built a Shopify store, set up my Facebook page, and ran ads to it."

However, after spending thousands of dollars on ads, I couldn't make a single dime.

I was puzzled. Why was my product not selling on Facebook but made a solid profit on Amazon.com? I started to research how some big brands crush it on social media, and I realized this:

When people search on Amazon.com, they already know what they want and **are ready to buy**. And they trust Amazon can deliver the product they purchased.

But when they are on social media, like browsing on Facebook, they have no awareness of my product, my brand, or have any reason to trust me.

That is why selling on Amazon can be so different from selling on another place.

So, I decided to stick with Amazon.

Then I got an email from Amazon. They told me my account was suspended because I sourced a patented product. They said I could no longer use their marketing channel.

With more than 4000 units of inventory in the warehouse, I panicked. I had to decide how to get rid of my stock!

Amazon gave me a deadline to remove my inventory. I could either choose to dispose of it or figure out a way to sell out before the deadline.

I ran ads, posted to groups, and tried to list my products on eBay. But no. I could not sell any.

I ended up disposing of all $20,000 worth of inventory, my entire year's revenue.

It was a painful and harsh lesson in my life.

And since I could no longer sell on Amazon, I needed to figure out another way to go forward. One question that came to my mind was, "How can someone build a successful e-com brand without Amazon?"

I started to study the top performers in the market and discovered almost all top sellers were doing the same thing.

They all had a **marketing funnel** – a system and process to convert their social media followers and website visitors into their customers.

Here is the brutal truth. It is unlikely someone will become your client immediately after following your Facebook page. Likewise, it is unlikely someone will book an appointment directly when they first land on your website or blog.

Most of the time, your potential clients need to go through a process, a **customer journey** to become your actual clients.

We called the process a **marketing funnel.**

Most businesses do not have this process in place. That's why they struggle with marketing.

A marketing funnel is a system that combines all of your digital assets–your website, your ads, your social media profile–to work together to **turn your audience into your clients** who go from becoming aware of the problem to booking an appointment.

A marketing funnel is broken up into four stages:

1. Awareness
2. Consideration
3. Decision
4. Action

Awareness

When your prospects are browsing the internet, they have little awareness who you are and what you do. In fact, they may have little insight about their problem.

To turn these people into clients, you need to bring awareness to them and educate them about your brand and offers.

You can do this by posting educational content on your social media or website.

There are 3 types of awareness you can communicate to your audience:

- The awareness of problems
- The awareness of the solution
- The awareness of you and your business

The key here is **"content."** Content is the tool we use to bring awareness to our prospects. That's why "information" was discussed in depth in the previous chapter.

As you saw, there are many different types of content you can publish to help your potential clients build awareness.

- You can post educational content on social media and blogs to build problem awareness and solution awareness.
- You can post a personal or brand story to build brand awareness.

Consideration

When your audience is aware of that potential problem, they will consider finding an expert to help them. They will either follow your pages, go to your website, ask questions on your fan page, or simply go to Google looking for a realtor.

Those are people who raised their hand and said, "I need some help. Tell me more."

The key here is **following up**. One study showed it takes seven touches for a prospect to become your client. You can do it with email marketing, retargeting ads, or even by phone.

- You can invite them to subscribe to your email newsletter for more information and follow up with them with helpful tips and call to action.
- You can run retargeting ads on social media and Google to remind them of their problem.

Decision

This is the point your prospects decide to hire someone and do all the research to find the best option

- They may search "real estate agent near me," "realty companies in New York," or other keywords to see all the candidates.
- They may read the review on your Google My Business Profile.
- They will check your social media profile and read the reviews of your existing clients.
- Or, if you have done a good job building a relationship with them in the previous two stages, they may just contact you since they remember your brand.

The key to all this is **"optimization."** You must optimize your website, Google my Business profile, and social media to stay at the forefront of people's minds.

- Optimize your social media and collect some five stars reviews.
- Optimize your Google My Business profile to show you are offering top-notch services.
- Optimize your website so it gets featured on search results.

Action

The last stage is action. It's the time your prospect decides to book an appointment and become your client. They will either go to your social media profile or your website to book an appointment with you.

The goal here is "seamlessness." Your audience should be able to find your website effortlessly, as well as your phone number and email address without much effort.

You can make booking an appointment with you a seamless process too by doing the following:

- Run Google ads that target your brand keyword so you won't miss any potential appointments when they look for your information.
- Make sure your homepage is optimized. People should find your phone number or email address without scrolling the website.
- Send an SMS reminder or a reminder call before the meeting.

A Simple Funnel Example

You can create a simple funnel with your social media and your website.

For example, you can use social media content to bring **awareness** to your audience. When people are aware, they will click on your website if they **consider** hiring you. You can then run retargeting ads to them to follow up and show them testimonials of your existing clients that remind them of their pain.

After visiting your website and consuming the content, they will **decide** whether they want to book an appointment with you. If not, they leave. If they are still interested, they continue exploring the site and **act**.

The same thing can be done with email marketing. It is another way to bring people through the funnel.

How Realtors Use Email Marketing to Generate New Clients

A funnel has a wider opening at the top, and then it shrinks as it goes down, like an inverted triangle. The idea is to fill the top with as many qualified people as possible. Then as you move them through your marketing tactics, the ones that will convert will remain.

The easiest way to explain this concept is in a real-life explanation.

Mr. Smith sees clients who need these services:

- Sell a houses
- Buy a new home
- Rent a home

His marketing plan is to bring as many people living in NYC to his website as possible.

He brings people to his website by not only posting on social media about real estate but also giving information about what is going on in NYC that would interest locals.

As Mr. Smith posts this information, he sees that he is gaining much attention from all types of people. To capture the people from social media, he creates an **opt-in page** to convert visitors to an email list.

An opt-in page is a particular type of web page that gives away freebies to collect a prospect's email address. This freebie can be a free report, a free buyers guide, free evaluation, or even a physical gift. People have to leave their email addresses to get those freebies.

So he wrote a free report about buying a home in NYC and ran a giveaway campaign on his social media. People who get interested in buying a home in NYC will sign up and become subscribers.

Our realtor takes this idea and does the same on his blog. He started publishing valuable content on his blog and invited his blog visitors to download his free report and sign up for his newsletter.

As he created more and more content on his social media and blog, he gets more and more website visitors and email subscribers.

Now that he has a great way to turn the audience into his subscribers, it is time to invite his subscribers to book an appointment with him.

He created an email marketing campaign.

He sent emails to build a relationship with his subscribers.

Some emails will provide educational content, some will share industry news, and others will share tips about buying and selling houses.

Once the general information has been delivered, the emails become more specific and action-oriented.

People will either convert or unsubscribe – some will simply stay on the email list, and that is okay. Those people may need more time to convert.

As the emails are sent, the marketing that was started will continue because that's what brings people into the funnel and converts the ones who can be converted.

The idea is to get as many people into the funnel as possible and then weed them out depending on whether they are interested. Now, when we say get as many people as possible, we mean people who are considered quality leads. Those people are the ones who are living or working in NYC.

Those are the people who may need your services.

Two Journeys for Customers

As you may have noticed, not every prospect becomes your client the same way. Different clients will go through different customer journeys. Usually, there are two common ways for someone to become your client.

#1. The Passive Approach

With this approach, you only market to those who are in the consideration or decision stage and try to convert those "low-hanging fruits" into your client.

Here is what the customer journey looks like:

1. **Awareness:** Your prospects want buy a house.
2. **Consideration:** They need help. And they start considering hiring a realtor.
3. **Decision:** They go to Google to look for a realtor and find your website.
4. **Action:** They compare different options and choose one to book an appointment.

You can reach these types of clients by search engine optimization, Google ads, and Google my Business optimization.

#2. The Active Approach

With this approach, you build a relationship with your prospects and educate them about the potential problem before they even consider hiring an agent.

In other words, you market to those who are unaware of the problem and bring them through the four stages.

Here is how the customer journey looks:

- **Awareness:** They read an article about selling or buying a home from your website or social media.

- **Consideration:** Consider booking an appointment with you.
- **Decision:** They email you or call you to ask questions, or they may do some research online.
- **Action:** They book an appointment with you.

You can reach this type of audience from social media, blogs, or email marketing.

It will take longer for you to convert this audience, but once you establish a relationship with them, they will remember you and become your lifetime clients.

These are just two types of ideal customer journeys. Of course, clients make decisions differently in real life. That is why it is important to utilize various media to reach out to people who are in the indifferent stage.

Getting Help with Feeding Your Funnel

This is a continuous marketing method. You cannot stop funneling the top because if you do, it will run dry, and you'll stop getting new clients. You don't want that to happen, especially when you've been so successful with everything you've done with your marketing.

Since you are a busy realtor running and growing your business, you likely need someone to help with feeding your funnel. That's why we are here. We help you bring in new clients continuously, so you can focus on providing the services. We devised this marketing strategy and have tested it on many businesses to make sure it works. And it does work!

If you are tired or worried about not getting new clients every month, it's time to use a different marketing method – a proven one that will help you finally breathe easier knowing that your business will survive despite the competition that surrounds it.

No matter if you're in NYC or Montgomery, Alabama, this strategy works and will help you.

Contact us on https://soldouthouses.com today to discuss how we can help you with your online marketing for your business. We use the S.W.I.F.T. method, which again is social media, website, information, funneling, and then traffic. This method has been devised by us, so we are the experts on it.

If you decide to try this yourself, you can use Clickfunnels. This platform will help you create the opt-in pages that will take people just browsing your website to your email list so you can bring them closer to becoming new clients.

They provide a free trial to try them out. If you decide to continue using it, you can buy the subscription. We use this platform, and it's been a game-changer in bringing qualified leads to our clients and us.

You can go to https://getCFfreetrial.com to sign up for your Clickfunnels free trial.

Now you know the funneling part of the S.W.I.F.T. method. The last part is Traffic. When you have the traffic, you have exactly what you need to generate new clients on a consistent basis.

TRAFFIC

The only way to bring in new clients on a consistent basis is to continue marketing to people in the area where your realty office is located.

With so many people living and working around your realty office, it can take years to reach them all. And the more your brand is put out into the community, the more likely people will convert.

In digital marketing, "traffic" means the visitors to your website and social media page.

There are two ways to generate visitors to your website in the internet marketing world.

Paid Traffic vs. Organic Traffic

Paid traffic is the fastest way to get access to your potential clients from the internet. By paying Facebook, Google, or other platforms, you can easily reach out to more audiences.

On the contrary, organic traffic is the **traffic you earn** by publishing high-quality content.

As I mentioned before, Content is King. Most websites will reward you with more traffic if you publish great content.

For example, if you publish a viral video on Facebook, it will be shared and reach millions of audiences.

If you publish a great article on your blog and it gets shared on many websites, you can easily get ranked on Google and reach more audiences.

That is why content is king. SEO is critical when it comes to digital marketing.

Since we already covered SEO and content marketing in previous chapters, in this chapter, I will focus on how you can get more traffic using paid advertising.

Take Advantage of Paid Traffic

Besides SEO and content marketing, there are many other ways to bring traffic to your website. Paid advertising is available on Google's search engine and Facebook.

When you pay to advertise on these platforms, you are paying to show your website/landing page to a specific audience.

Know Your Numbers

If you want to buy ads, the first thing to keep in mind is **knowing your numbers.**

The biggest issue with traditional marketing is that it's hard to track and hard to optimize – businesses may spend millions on a TV commercial, newsletters, and flyers. Still, when clients come, they have no clue what marketing campaign works, and they end up wasting lots of money on underperforming ads.

The most significant advantage of internet marketing is its trackability- you can install a code on your site, and suddenly, everything becomes transparent.

There are two types of numbers to keep your eyes on.

The first type is your ad cost. They are:

- **CPC** (pay per click) – how much you spend on average to get a click
- **CPL** (pay per lead) – how much you spend on average to get an appointment or a lead
- **CPA** (cost per acquisition) – how much you spend to acquire a new client

Another type of number is your customer value. They are

- **ACV** (average customer value) – How much on average a client will spend on your service their first visit
- **LTV** (customer lifetime value) – How much on average a client will spend on your service in their entire life

The key to profit from paid ads is to optimize ad creatives and get the lowest CPA (cost per acquisition) possible and to maximize your service and funnel to get the highest LTV (customer lifetime value) possible.

When your LTV > CPA, your business grows; otherwise, you will struggle.

Use Split Testing to Optimize Your Ads

One of the most common methods to optimize your ads is "split testing." You create multiple ads on each campaign and let the system deliver its impression or traffic evenly to those ads.

Over time, you will notice some ads get more engagement, and some bring you more clients.

You then turn off the underperforming ads and create more variations to challenge the existing winner.

Over time, your ads will perform better and better.

Split testing is a robust process since it can help you lower your CPA and get a higher ROI (return on investment) from your ad campaign.

Turn Your Leads into Lifetime Clients

Two major factors determine the ad costs: supply and demand. The more competitors you have, the higher ad cost you need to pay.

And the ad cost is not something you can control. You can optimize your ads, but there is always a limit.

That is why you not only need to optimize your ads but also try your best to turn every lead into a lifetime customer.

The longer they stick with you, the more profit you can make and the more value you can bring to their life.

The key here is relatively simple – provide excellent service and make your clients satisfied.

No marketing tricks can compensate for poor service.

I know there are many marketing tricks about maximum customer's lifetime value like upsell and cross-sell, and yes, I used to pay a lot of money to some gurus because of those tricks. Still, I canceled many of the programs I bought from them because I saw no value in them.

Your ad can help you win an appointment.

But only excellent service can help you win a lifetime client.

Which Types of Ads Can You Use?

There are different social media platforms you can use to run your ads. But here we tell you the best ones to get efficient results with less effort. So have a look at these different ad types.

#1. Search Ads:

The most common type of ad is the search ads. On the Google search results page, you can see these ads. It is a type of pay-per-click ad.

By using these ads, advertisers only pay money when users click on the ads.

By clicking on the ads, the user is redirected to the main website and helps the user to make an appointment with the real estate agent. These ads appear on the top and bottom of the website with the **highlight** *"Ad."*

This is so you can make a distinction between a website and an ad. These ads contain text instead of videos and images. By using Google ads, you can set up your search ads.

Google Ads

Google ads are the ones that display on the Google search results page.

This is one of the most utilized paid Google advertising options available today. You can use Google ads to set up your campaign by choosing the keywords your target audience uses in a search and then creating an ad that attracts people to click through to your website.

It's important to know which keyword phrases will work best for your ad and the type of ad that will make your target audience click.

You must also know when the best times are to display your ads for the best results.

There are two main types of Google ads that you usually see.

- Local Ads
- International Ads

The main purpose of local advertising is to attract a local audience. In these ads, advertisers usually focus on the people who live near to the workplace.

International ads are made to attract a foreign audience.

Google ads use a specific algorithm to target the audience according to their income. To target the specific audience, you need to edit your ads by clicking on the "Advanced Location."

- After clicking on the option, a menu will pop up.
- Here select the "Location Groups" tab. Then the list with three options will appear.
- Select the demographics option from the list.
- Now, select the income tier in which you have an interest. Click on the ad button.

By making these changes, you can target the wealthy audience who wants to sell or buy a house.

You can use the following tricks to enhance the results of Google ads.

How to Set Up a Search Ad

The first thing is to select the right keywords for your search ad. The right use of keywords helps your ads to appear in the top positions of Google search results.

If you want to promote your services to the right people, then make sure you use the relevant location and brand keywords in the ad content.

Otherwise, with the wrong use of keywords, only the wrong audience will go to your page.

For **PPC ads,** long-tail keywords work best. These keywords have more than one important word in them. They also attract more audiences at a low cost per click.

Before you use the keywords, you need to enter the auction and bid for the keyword that relates to your content. If you place a high bid, you will get the right to use this specific keyword in your ads.

Your bidding amount and the quality of the content determine whether you get the keyword or not.

Your quality score decides the position of your website. To increase the quality, all you can do is write creative and better content for ads.

Once you get the keyword, you can launch your PPC search ad. It is the most common type of advertising that most people view during google searches.

#2. Display Ads:

The other type of PPC ad is the display ad. You can use these ads to attract people that have an interest in your business. Unlike search ads, these ads have images with text.

Instead of appearing on the Google search results page, these ads appear on the partner websites.

By using display ads, you can easily target the interested audience and provide them with your best services.

You can also set your target market and display ads to the people who visit your website.

How to Set Up a Display Ad

Like other PPC ads, you need to bid for these ads in the auction. Here you select the amount that you pay when the user clicks on it.

To use the display ad, you need approval from Google for your ad copy. To make sure your ad does not get denied, you can follow Google's Ad Image Requirements.

After getting approval from Google, the next step is to select a real estate industry-related website.

This is so you can attract an organic audience. If you select some other famous website, then uninterested people will come to your website.

These ads run on a PPC CPC model. Most people do not click these ads. But they still help in promoting the content to the people. Display ads have more potential to attract users.

Use the appropriate picture to display with the ads. That way people can see the actual services instead of getting confused about your services.

#3. Social Ads:

The most famous type of advertising is social ads. Since most people use social media, it is easy to grab their attention to your ads.

Also, social media can be used on all devices like mobile phones, **MAC, tablets,** and **PCs.**

Social ads also display on all devices. It helps a large audience to see the ads, and they can navigate to the original website. By using social ads, you can stay in contact with your customers easily.

How You Can Set Up a Social Media Ad

Before using the social media ad, you must select the platform on which you want to promote your content. Following are the common social media platforms we're all familiar with.

- *Facebook*
- *Twitter*
- *Instagram*
- *YouTube*
- *LinkedIn*
- *Pinterest*

By using any of these platforms, you can reach the maximum audience. Remember that each platform has a different format. So it is important to choose one that seems convenient to you.

Make sure to use the right images that you want to post. Remember that posts should be related to your brand or service. It will help you in doing the right marketing.

These ads are also paid ads. To reach a large audience, you need to boost your posts.

According to your range, you can select the boosting type. The results totally depend on the amount that you spend on ads.

Social media helps you to target specific people. They use the following factors to define the audience.

- *Location*
- *Behaviors*
- *Demographics*
- *Interest*
- *Education*

By using these factors, you can easily target interested users without wasting your money. If you use all social media, then you can promote your services on a wide scale.

1. Facebook Ads:

Facebook is one of the most widely used advertising options. Here, you can have ads come up in people's feeds.

When setting up your ad campaign, you identify which audience you want – age, location, interests, etc. This way, your ad isn't shown to people uninterested in what you're promoting.

Due to the easy interface of Facebook, most people prefer to use it. Instead of using this platform as a source of entertainment, you should do marketing here.

By creating a business page on Facebook, you can create ads. All you need is to select the right boosting package to make your posts visible to a large audience.

If you do not have advertising knowledge, then start with the low package. When you start getting the appropriate and expected results, you can change the promotion package.

Your ads will display to many people between their posts. If they have an interest in your services, then they will surely come to your page.

2. Instagram Ads:

After Facebook, Instagram is the best social media platform. The format differs a bit from Facebook.

Here, people prefer to post images instead of videos.

While creating the ad, make sure to upload the picture that relates to your brand, services, and offers.

Do not upload random pictures because it can confuse people. In the caption section, write every single detail about your services.

This way people do not have to come to your page and can navigate to the right information. Just as you use keywords in search ads, here you can use the right hashtags.

They will help in boosting your post in places like Facebook. You also have to select a promotion plan on Instagram. According to your boosting plan, Instagram automatically displays your posts on the user's homepage.

To make a distinction between simple posts and ad posts, **Instagram displays** *"Ad"* on the post. By clicking on the post, the user redirects to the official page.

3. YouTube Ads:

The format of YouTube is completely different from Instagram and Facebook. Here you need to upload videos instead of pictures. Also, you make a channel instead of a page for advertising.

You can use both skippable and non-skippable ads in other people's videos. The skippable ads are the ones that you can skip after 5 sec. The total length of these videos can be 2 to 3 minutes.

You have to pay for the ad if the user sees your ad full time. But if they skip after 5 sec, you will not be charged.

However, as the name says, you can not skip the non-skippable ads. You have to watch them even if you do not want to.

The total length of these ads varies from 5 secs to 10 secs so that people do not get bored. These ads can be displayed at the start, in the middle, or at the end of the video.

4. Remarketing Ads:

The best PPC ad is the remarketing ad. You can use this ad when you want to attract an interested audience. It helps in generating leads by providing more conversion.

Due to the social media promotion, you can get most people on your website. But they don't need to end up making an appointment.

They can just review your services and know about your experience, and then leave.

You have no control over whether users make an appointment. All you can do here is use remarketing ads because they help engage the audience.

When users visit your website for the first time, these ads automatically display on the page. Usually, the ads contain the best offers and services you provide.

These ads do not disappear until the user clicks on them. By clicking on the ad, users are usually redirected to a make-an-appointment page or the login page.

To engage your customer, it is considered better to add the email field in the login form. This way you can email your customers about new services and offers or inform them about things that concern them like changes to hours or upcoming events.

How to Set Up a Remarketing Ad

To run successful remarketing ads requires a **tracking pixel.** It is Google's remarketing code. If you already use **PPC ads**, then you can add this tracking pixel to your advertising campaign.

By using the tracking pixel, you can analyze what your audience sees on your page. This way you can determine what services and offers your audience likes the best.

According to their searching, users are categorized in the proper lists. To segment your audience, you must make different lists to run your ads.

After the listing, people only see the ads of the services and offers in which they have an interest. The main purpose of remarketing ads is to focus on the products and the service that people view the most.

By displaying these specific ads, you can keep your audience engaged. It increases the conversion rate by providing people with what they want.

5. Click-to-Call Ads:

To make your ad effective, you can add the call facility to it. It appears like a call icon that you can add to your Google ads. This option helps people to contact you directly.

This saves time and makes your ads more efficient. Make sure to use your active mobile number to respond to your clients within a short time.

This feature is not available for the people who access Google from their mobile phones since PCs and mobile phones have different formats. So mobile users will have difficulty navigating through the ad easily.

6. Call-Only Ads:

These ads are the alternative to simple click-to-call ads. By using call-only ads, you can design ads for all who use mobile, PC, or laptop.

If you use click-to-call ads, then mobile users will find it difficult to contact you this way. They will leave your ad and just go to the next realtor.

You can avoid this problem by using call-only ads. Always remember your main purpose is to facilitate the most people by giving them easy access to your information.

7. Google Map Ads:

Google maps show the registered places with their directions. This way people can easily reach their destinations without wasting time and getting confused.

To add your business to Google maps, you need to make a Google My Business account. While creating the business account, you need to enter the following information:

- *Brand Name*
- *Location*
- *Working Hours*
- *Services*
- *Phone Number*
- *Experience*

Without entering this information, you will not be able to sign up easily. Once your business profile is created, you can see your brand on Google maps with directions.

This feature helps people reach your workplace after they make an appointment with you. Google maps also gives notifications to people when they are near your workplace.

Other Ways to Send Traffic to Your Website

Traffic is what will keep your funnel alive, so it's important to continuously come up with ways to build traffic.

You now know you can gain traffic from SEO, social media, Google ads and Facebook ads, but there are many other ways to bring even more traffic.

For instance, you can encourage current clients to share your website with their friends and family.

This will help you bring in the people who are not online as much as others are. You can also advertise your website in your community. The more people see you in newspapers, at community events, and other areas, the more likely they will be to come to your website and join your email marketing list.

You can bring more people to your website by promoting it on other websites too. You can ask other websites if you can guest post on their blog with a link back to your site. You can also simply ask to put a link to your site on their website.

When you do this, more people will see your link and click on it. Just be sure the websites you're putting your link on have the same audience you want to attract. For example, if you're a realtor in Los Angeles, you want your website address on sites that many LA residents visit.

Traffic is the heart and soul of your marketing. It is how you keep your funnel full. When you can keep the traffic flowing, you can keep new clients coming in.

The S.W.I.F.T. method of marketing your real estate business is effective. If you use this strategy for your business, you will see results from it. You need to follow all the steps, though.

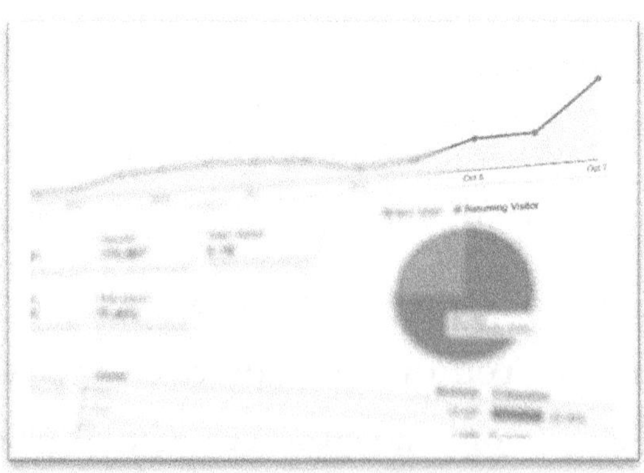

CONTACT US FOR HELP WITH GENERATING TRAFFIC

We can help you generate enough traffic to keep your funnel full. We have devised the S.W.I.F.T. method that effectively brings traffic to a site to a conversion funnel. THIS is the way we have been able to help many real estate agents grow their business to achieve great success.

You should not have to struggle to bring in new clients every month. When you have the right type of marketing in place, new clients should come to you regularly without you having to do much at all except take care of the clients.

If you're having a difficult time with online marketing, contact us. We can take the entire process off your hands so you can concentrate on what matters – providing quality services to your clients.

For more information on how our services help real estate agents nationwide, contact us at https://soldouthouses.com today.

Our services are affordable, effective, and will pay for themselves when you receive new clients because of our proven method.

SPECIAL BONUS: WOULD YOU LIKE OUR TEAM TO DESIGN A CUSTOM MARKETING PLAN FOR YOU FREE?

Thanks for making it to the end. I hope you enjoyed this book so far.

Now you have the framework of how we market our business. The next question you might have is

"How do I customize it for my local business?"

That's the reason I want to provide you with a 1-on-1 strategy call For Free.

What You Will Get:

One of our marketing experts will meet with you live using Skype and literally design a customized marketing plan specifically for your business.

Once it's designed, we'll then build you a blueprint and a process map so you'll be able to deploy it at will.

Here's How It Works:

We begin working before we ever meet.

First, you must complete an application form and tell us about your business.

We analyze your target market, spy on your competitors, and play "mystery prospects" by going through your website, fan page, and content as if we were a potential client.

Then We Meet, One-On-One.

We'll do it using Skype or phone, and we will discuss with you the things that need to be changed to attract more leads to you.

Everything is custom and is designed specifically for your business after we've had a chance to ask you about your marketing process, your revenue goals, and your branding strategy.

There Is No Charge For This, and There Is No Catch.

...Which, of course, leads you to wonder, "Why would you do all of this work for free?"

Well, in the interest of full transparency, this is how I get clients.

A good percentage of the people I do this for end up asking us to actually create their website, build their sales funnel, write all their content, and set up marketing campaigns for them.

When that happens, my team and I actually build all the web pages, build the follow-up campaigns, write the content, set up ads, and implement everything <u>for</u> the client.

So that's my "hidden motivation" for doing this. However ...

This Is NOT A "Sales Pitch In Disguise"

Far from it.

You'll get no pressure to become a client because we let the value of the free work speak for itself.

The marketing plan we design for you, for free, will be absolutely transformative to your business.

I guarantee it.

The bottom line is we'll design an amazing marketing plan for free, and we'll even give you a blueprint of it so you can deploy it at once.

After that, you might want to become a client. Or not.

I won't pressure you either way.

If you'd like a free customized marketing plan and blueprint, click the link below to get started.

Go to
https://call.soldouthouses.com/
to book your free strategy call.

RESOURCES

Thanks for reading this book. The following are some resources that can help you take your real estate business to the next level

1. The Ultimate Real Estate Marketing Checklist (Free)

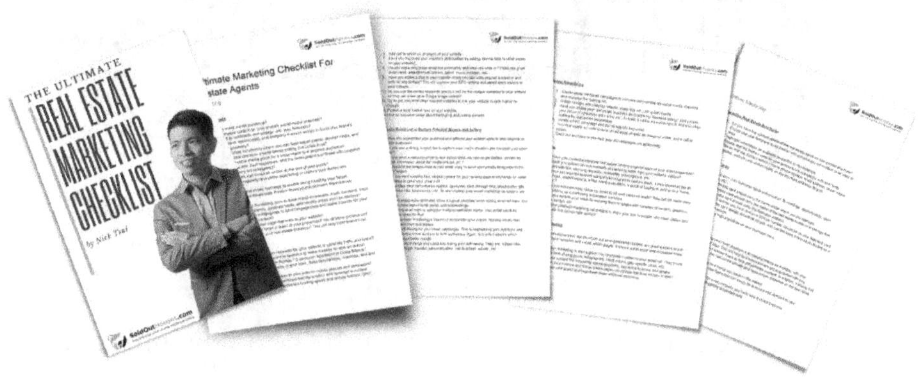

Get 86 proven real estate marketing ideas to
generate more leads online.

Please go to https://soldouthouses.com/checklist
to download your free checklist.

2. Our Digital Marketing Services

Want my team to take care of your internet marketing for you?

Visit our site at https://services.soldouthouses.com/ to see what you can do to bring your real estate marketing to the next level.

3. 150 Done-for-You Real Estate Infographics

Get your social media content ready in the next few minutes.

You can get your infographic package at https://soldouthouses.com/infographics.

4. 360 Real Estate Social Media Post Templates

Create professional social media content quickly
with these templates.

You can get the templates at
https://soldouthouses.com/socialmediaposttemplates .

5. 360 Real Estate Ad Templates

Create professional social media ad images quickly with these templates.

You can get all templates at
https://soldouthouses.com/adtemplates

6. Ebook - 3-Minute Real Estate Ads

Get 30 done-for-you social media ad copy swipe files for a huge discount.

You can grab your copy at https://soldouthouses.com/3minads .

7. Our Sold Out Houses Pro Membership

Would you like to get access to 1700+ real estate marketing tools & templates for less than the price of a toca per day? Our membership provides you all the tools and templates you need to succeed with real estate marketing, and you can try it for 100% free today.

Go to https://soldouthouses.com/vip to claim your 14-day free trial.